MW00699782

Science Vocabulary Building

Grades 3–5

BY
SCHYRLET CAMERON AND CAROLYN CRAIG

COPYRIGHT © 2009 Mark Twain Media, Inc.

ISBN 978-1-58037-490-3

Printing No. CD-404109

Mark Twain Media, Inc., Publishers
Distributed by Carson-Dellosa Publishing Company, Inc.

Visit us at www.carsondellosa.com

Table of Contents

Introduction to the Teacher

Science Vocabulary Building is intended to help students learn terms that are important to the content taught in science. The International Reading Association promotes teaching vocabulary to improve comprehension. As a goal, the National Research Council, organized by the National Academy of Science, has established that all students should achieve scientific literacy. An essential aspect of scientific literacy is gaining a greater knowledge of the subject matter associated with physical, life, and earth science. Providing vocabulary instruction is one of the most significant ways a teacher can promote student understanding and academic achievement in science.

As students progress through grades three, four, five, and beyond, reading science content becomes progressively more problematic. There is a significant increase in the number of words with three or more syllables. Those students who are skillful in reading these multisyllabic words can read for comprehension without the challenge of word pronunciation. Learning to read these words and understand their meanings increases the readability level for all students.

National and state science standards, science textbooks, and Mark Twain Media science publications were reviewed in an effort to identify commonly used science words for each grade level. This book focuses on teaching these high-utility terms. Words are listed in alphabetical order. Each entry provides the learner with pronunciation and syllabication information to help the student with decoding. The entry also provides a definition and uses the word in context to help the students gain an understanding of the meaning of the word.

The teaching strategies described in this book promote differentiated instruction. Vocabulary building activities provide multiple opportunities for students to learn the language of science. Alternative methods of instruction, such as hands-on activities, small group work, games, and journaling, target multiple learning styles and help learners at all levels. Teachers may choose to focus on decoding and word meanings for English-language learners and reluctant readers. Challenging activities provide all students with opportunities for extended learning.

The instructional activities found in this book are designed to promote scientific literacy through vocabulary learning. They can be used as stand-alone units or to supplement and enrich the content area. Each section includes:

- **Alphabetized Word List:** a glossary of high-utility science terms with pronunciation and syllabication sections presented in an easy-to-read and understand format
- **Vocabulary Building Activities:** provide students with multiple opportunities to learn and use the term
- **Vocabulary Games:** provide meaningful reinforcement of new terms
- **Interactive Vocabulary Building Websites:** provide students with enrichment opportunities

Science Vocabulary Building supports the No Child Left Behind (NCLB) Act. The book promotes student knowledge and understanding of science and mathematics concepts through vocabulary building. The activities are designed to strengthen scientific literacy skills and are correlated to the National Science Education Standards (NSES) and the National Council for Teachers of Mathematics Standards (NCTM).

National Standards

> **National Science Education Standards (NSES)**
> National Research Council (1996). *National Science Education Standards.*
> Washington, D.C.: National Academy Press.

Science as Inquiry
- Content Standard A: As a result of activities in grades 3–5, all students should develop abilities necessary to do scientific inquiry.
- Content Standard A: As a result of activities in grades 3–5, all students should develop understanding about scientific inquiry.

Physical Science
- Content Standard B: As a result of activities in grades 3–4, all students should develop understanding of properties of objects and materials, position and motion of objects, and light, heat, electricity, and magnetism.
- Content Standard B: As a result of activities in grade 5, all students should develop understanding of properties of objects and materials, motions and of forces, and transfer of energy.

Life Science
- Content Standard C: As a result of activities in grades 3–4, all students should develop understanding of the characteristics of organisms, life cycles of organisms, and organisms and environments.
- Content Standard C: As a result of activities in grade 5, all students should develop understanding of structure and function in living systems and adaptations of organisms.

Earth and Space Science
- Content Standard D: As a result of activities in grades 3–4, all students should develop understanding of properties of earth materials, objects in the sky, and changes in earth and sky.
- Content Standard D: As a result of activities in grade 5, all students should develop understanding of structure of the earth system, Earth's history, and Earth in the solar system.

> **National Council for Teachers of Mathematics Standards (NCTM)**
> National Council for Teachers of Mathematics (2000). *Principles and Standards for School Mathematics.* Reston, VA: National Council for Teachers of Mathematics.

Measurement
- In grades 3–5, students should be able to understand measurable attributes of objects and the units, systems, and processes of measurement.
- In grades 3–5, students should be able to apply appropriate techniques, tools, and formulas to determine measurements.

How to Use This Book

Science reading materials present students with new and often difficult words. If students do not know the meaning of a sufficient proportion of the words in the reading material, they may become frustrated and skip important words, which can make understanding the text difficult. Teaching science vocabulary first will help students build an understanding of the concepts to be taught. The Association for Supervision and Curriculum Development and International Reading Association support using a systematic approach to teaching vocabulary.

Strategies

- Focus on the most important words.
- Provide students with a science-rich environment where they see, hear, read, and speak the new vocabulary words multiple times.
- Have students record word meanings, experiment results, and answers to activities in their science journals. This will provide a review resource for the students and an assessment tool for teachers and parents.

Word Wall

cell	consumer
chloroplast	decomposer
cytoplasm	environment
enzyme	habitat
nucleus	niche
osmosis	predator
organelle	organism

Display words on a bulletin board.

Teaching Science Vocabulary

Step #1–Introduce Words: The teacher reads the word and discusses the information provided in the vocabulary chart.

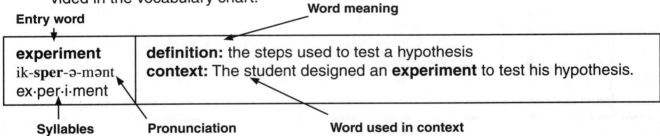

Entry word

Word meaning

| **experiment**
ik-**sper**-ə-mənt
ex·per·i·ment | **definition:** the steps used to test a hypothesis
context: The student designed an **experiment** to test his hypothesis. |

Syllables　　　Pronunciation　　　Word used in context

Step #2–Construct Meaning: Students construct their own meaning, write a sentence, and create a visual representation of the word in their science journals.

Word	Definition	Picture
	Sentence	

Step #3–Practice Using the Word: Students gain more knowledge of the words by participating in science activities provided with each word list.

Step #4–Reinforcement: Students participate in a variety of reinforcement activities, such as hangman and charades, to strengthen what they have learned.

Pronunciation Key

What Is a Pronunciation Key?

It is often hard to tell from the spelling of a word how it should be pronounced. A special alphabet of symbols is used to indicate the sounds spoken in the pronunciation of words. A pronunciation key is a list of these symbols and familiar words that contain the sound represented by the symbols.

Pronunciation symbols and their keys differ slightly among various dictionaries and science books. The system used in this book was especially designed to make it easier for you to read and understand the written pronunciations. Place a copy of the key below in your science journal as a quick reference for the pronunciation symbols used in this book.

Using a Pronunciation Key

- Symbols are used to represent the sounds used in the pronunciation of a word.
- Hyphens (-) are used to separate the pronunciations into syllables.
- **Boldface** letters are used to indicate the part of the word to be stressed or spoken with the greatest force.
- In the syllabication listing, dots (·) are used to separate the word into syllables.

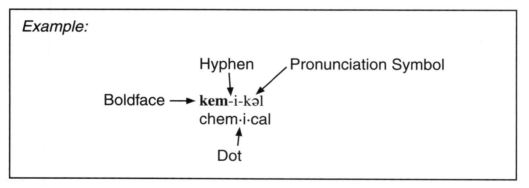

Example:

Hyphen   Pronunciation Symbol

Boldface ⟶ **kem**-i-kəl

chem·i·cal

Dot

Pronunciation Key

a	lap, pat, mad	o	hot, top, odd
ā	lane, age, hay	ō	old, toad, know, toe
ä	father, yarn, ah	oi	oil, toy
âr	care, hair	ô	law, caught, for, horse, off, order
e	bet, end, hen, said	o͝o	book, pull, should
ē	bee, equal, piece, real	o͞o	fruit, glue, food, few
ər	better, perfect, baker	ou	out, cow, house
ə	about, taken, pencil, come, circus	sh	she, dish, machine
hw	when, whether, nowhere	th	thin, both
i	kit, in	*th*	this, mother, smooth
ī	ice, my, line, cried	u	cut, up
îr	ear, deer, here, pierce	ûr	fur, term, bird, word, learn

Science Journal

Directions: Complete the vocabulary chart below. Copy the word, make your own definition, write a sentence, and create a picture for the word. Collect all your science journal pages in a binder or folder to use as a reference.

Word	Definition	Picture
	Sentence	
Word	Definition	Picture
	Sentence	
Word	Definition	Picture
	Sentence	
Word	Definition	Picture
	Sentence	
Word	Definition	Picture
	Sentence	

Section 1.1: Scientific Method Word List

conclusion kən-**klōō**-zhən con·clu·sion	**definition:** the last part of an experiment where the findings are summarized **context:** The **conclusion** summarized the test results.
data **dā**-tə da·ta	**definition:** a group of measurements, facts, or statistics recorded about an experiment **context:** She graphed the **data** from the rock lab.
examine ig-**zam**-in ex·am·ine	**definition:** to look closely at someone or something **context:** **Examine** a small amount of sand with a microscope and record your observations.
experiment ik-**sper**-ə-mənt ex·per·i·ment	**definition:** the steps used to test a hypothesis **context:** The student designed an **experiment** to test his hypothesis.
hypothesis hī-**poth**-i-səs hy·poth·e·sis	**definition:** an idea about the solution to a problem that can be tested or investigated **context:** He designed an experiment to test his **hypothesis**.
identify ī-**den**-tə-fī i·den·ti·fy	**definition:** to name or recognize a person, place, or thing **context:** The student will **identify** the colors in a rainbow.
measure **mezh**-ər meas·ure	**definition:** to assign numbers to an observation such as length, mass, or volume **context:** **Measure** the length of your desk to the nearest centimeter.
observe əb-**zûrv** ob·serve	**definition:** to use the senses to gather information about an object or event **context:** **Observe** what the wind does to leaves, twigs, and other debris on the ground.
predict pri-**dikt** pre·dict	**definition:** a forecast of future events based on previous observations and experiments **context:** Using the data from the experiment, he could **predict** which patients were at risk of having a heart attack.
procedure prə-**sē**-jər pro·ce·dure	**definition:** a set of steps to follow to perform a specific task **context:** Students followed the **procedure** for the experiment.
record ri-**kôrd** re·cord	**definition:** to create an account of information for later use **context:** The scientist will **record** the data on a table.
research ri-**sûrch** re·search	**definition:** the method of collecting information and data about a topic being studied **context:** Students used their **research** to write a report.
scientific method sī-ən-tif-ik **meth**-əd sci·en·tif·ic meth·od	**definition:** a series of steps scientists use to solve a problem **context:** Students follow the **scientific method** when creating a science fair project.

Section 1.1: Vocabulary Building Activities

Scientific Method: Scientists ask questions about the world around them. They use the steps in the scientific method to explore possible answers. Students use the same steps when creating a science fair project. Design a poster that explains the steps.

Steps in the Scientific Method

1. Question: What do you want to learn from the experiment?
2. Hypothesis: What do you think will happen in the experiment?
3. Experiment: How will you test the hypothesis?
4. Data: What are the results of the experiment?
5. Conclusion: Do the results support your hypothesis?

Science Fair Project Topic: A good topic is one you can test with an experiment. It is important that the topic is not too broad.

Example:

Topic Too Broad	Good Topic
Worms	What do worms like to eat?

Decide which topics are good ideas for a science fair project.

1. the effect of fertilizer on plants
2. earthquakes in my state
3. types of popcorn
4. best brand of batteries

Write your own example of a good topic for a science fair project in your science journal.

The Big Question: Scientists ask questions about what they see going on in their world. They explain exactly what they want to learn from the scientific investigation by writing a question, called the "Big Question." After they have written the "Big Question," scientists predict what they will find. Scientists call this careful guess a hypothesis.

Practice writing a "Big Question" and hypothesis. An example has been provided.

Topic	Question	Hypothesis
plants	Does fertilizer effect plant growth?	Plants grow taller when given fertilizer.
paper towels		

Formulate a Conclusion: The concluding statement will either support or not support your original hypothesis.

Read the hypotheses and analyze the data below. Write a conclusion for the scientific investigation in your science journal.

Hypothesis: Flashlights run longer with "Ever Last" batteries.

Test Results

Brand	Starting Time	Stopping Time	Hours of Operation
Ever Last	3:00 P.M.	11:00 P.M.	8 hours
Mighty Power	3:00 P.M.	9:00 P.M.	6 hours
#1 Battery	3:00 P.M.	7:00 P.M.	4 hours

Section 1.2: Scientific Equipment Word List

anemometer an-ə-**mom**-i-tər an·e·mom·e·ter	**definition:** used to measure the wind speed in miles per hour **context:** The student placed an **anemometer** in the weather station to measure wind speed.	
balance scale **bal**-əns **skāl** bal·ance scale	**definition:** used to measure the mass in an object **context:** The **balance scale** was used to measure the mass of the apple.	
barometer bə-**räm**-ət-ər ba·rom·e·ter	**definition:** used to measure changes in air pressure **context:** When the **barometer** rises, it signals that cool, dry weather is on its way.	
beaker **bē**-kər bea·ker	**definition:** glass container used to hold liquids **context:** The student used the **beaker** to hold liquid for an experiment.	
coverslip **kəv**-ər-slip cov·er·slip	**definition:** used to flatten the object being viewed and to keep the microscope lens clean **context:** Place the **coverslip** over the drop of pond water to slow evaporation from the surface of the slide.	
forceps **fôr**-səps for·ceps	**definition:** used to pick up small objects **context:** The scientist used the **forceps** to hold the cotton thread over the flame of the Bunsen burner.	
graduated cylinder **graj**-o͞o-āt-ed **sil**-ən-dər grad·u·at·ed cyl·in·der	**definition:** used to make accurate measurements of liquid volumes **context:** Measure 10 milliliters of water in a **graduated cylinder**.	
magnet **mag**-nit mag·net	**definition:** used to attract or repel other objects made of iron or steel **context:** Use the **magnet** to pick up the iron filings.	
magnifying glass **mag**-nə-fī-ing **glas** mag·ni·fy·ing glass	**definition:** used to make objects appear larger **context:** The student used a **magnifying glass** to examine the mold growing on the white bread.	
medicine dropper **med**-i-sin **drop**-ər med·i·cine drop·per	**definition:** used to transfer small amounts of liquid **context:** Use the **medicine dropper** to add two drops of iodine to the test tube.	

Section 1.2: Scientific Equipment Word List (cont.)

microscope **mī**-krə-skōp mi·cro·scope	**definition:** used for viewing objects that are too small to be seen by the naked eye **context:** Use the **microscope** to observe the microorganisms in the pond water.	
microscope slide **mī**-krə-skōp **slīd** mi·cro·scope slide	**definition:** a narrow piece of glass used as a platform for viewing objects under the microscope **context:** The teacher used lens paper to clean the **microscope slide**.	
rain gauge **rān gāj** rain gauge	**definition:** used to measure how much rain has fallen **context:** Hold the **rain gauge** at eye level to get an accurate reading of how much rain has fallen.	
safety eyewear **sāf**-tē **ī**-wer safe·ty eye·wear	**definition:** used to prevent injury to the eye **context:** The teacher instructed the students to put on their **safety eyewear** before doing the lab work.	
spring scale **spring skāl** spring scale	**definition:** used to measure mass or force **context:** Use a **spring scale** to measure the amount of force needed to pull the brick across the table.	
telescope **tel**-ə-skōp te·le·scope	**definition:** used for viewing faraway objects, such as planets and stars **context:** The astronomer examined the craters of the moon using a **telescope**.	
10-cm ruler 10 **sen**-tə-mē-tər **rōō**-lər 10 cen·ti·me·ter rul·er	**definition:** used to measure length **context:** The **10-centimeter ruler** was used to measure the length of the ladybug.	
test tube **test tōōb** test tube	**definition:** used to hold or heat small amounts of liquid **context:** The student placed two drops of water in each **test tube**.	
test tube brush **test tōōb brəsh** test tube brush	**definition:** used to scrub glass pieces of equipment **context:** Use the **test tube brush** to clean the test tube used in the experiment.	
test tube rack **test tōōb rak** test tube rack	**definition:** used to hold several test tubes **context:** A **test tube rack** was used to hold the clean test tubes.	
thermometer thər-**mom**-i-tər ther·mom·e·ter	**definition:** used to determine temperature **context:** The student measured the temperature of the liquids using a **thermometer**.	
wind vane **wind vān** wind vane	**definition:** used to determine the direction the wind is blowing **context:** The meteorologists used a **wind vane** to measure wind direction.	

Section 1.2: Vocabulary Building Activities

Microscope Diagram

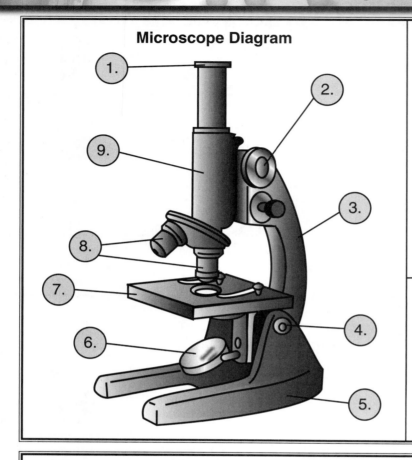

Microscope Diagram Directions: Using the word list below, identify the parts of the microscope in the diagram at the left. Record the answers in your science journal.

arm	base	mirror
stage	ocular lens	body tube

objective lenses

adjustment knob

stage adjustment knob

Online Resource: Learn more about using a microscope at the following website. "Microscope Parts." Utah State Office of Education. <http://www.usoe.k12.ut.us/curr/Science/sciber00/7th/cells/sciber/micrpart.htm>

Microscope Matching Directions: Match the microscope part with the job it does.

_____ 1. adjustment knob   _____ 6. stage

_____ 2. arm   _____ 7. objective lenses

_____ 3. base   _____ 8. ocular lens

_____ 4. mirror   _____ 9. body tube

_____ 5. stage adjustment

a. the upper lens or eyepiece of a microscope that the viewer looks through
b. the lower lens in a microscope that is closest to what is being looked at
c. used to raise or lower the body tube
d. used to support the body tube and stage
e. used to provide a firm, steady support
f. used to direct light through the opening in the stage and ocular lens
g. used to raise or lower the stage
h. a small platform on a microscope where the specimen is mounted for examination
i. used to hold the ocular lens and objective lenses

Section 1.2: Vocabulary Building Activities (cont.)

Meteorologists study the weather by recording and analyzing data. You can become an amateur meteorologist by building your own weather station and keeping a record of the measurements in your science journal.

Weather Journal: Each day, record the weather instrument measurements in your journal.

Thermometer: Place a thermometer outside, away from the building, and in the shade. When reading the temperature, hold the thermometer at eye level. Keep the thermometer out of the snow and rain.

Wind Vane: Cut the point and tail of an arrow out of an index card. Tape them to the ends of a straw. Push a pin through the middle of the straw. Stick the pin into the eraser of a pencil. Make sure the straw can turn freely. Take your wind vane outside. Hold the wind vane up in the air and face north. The arrow will point to the direction the wind is blowing from. Record wind direction in your weather journal.

Rain Gauge: Cut off the top third of a plastic pop bottle. Place some marbles in the bottom. The marbles will weigh down the bottle so that it won't tip over. Turn the top upside down and tape it inside the bottle. Pour water in the bottle to just cover the marbles. Tape a ruler to the side of the bottle starting with 0 at the base water level. Put the rain gauge outside on a level surface, away from any overhang or trees. Measure the rainfall every day at about the same time of day. To get an accurate reading, you must be at eye level with the top of the water. Record your measurements in your weather journal.

Barometer: Cut the neck off a balloon. Stretch the balloon tightly over the mouth of a jar or can. Secure the balloon with a rubber band or string. Make sure a flat, air-tight seal is formed on the jar or can. Tape one end of a straw to the middle of the balloon. Place the barometer inside, away from a window. When the air pressure is **high**, it will push in on the balloon, forming a dip. This will make the free end of the straw point **up**. This means fine weather is on the way. When the air pressure is **low**, the balloon will be puffed up and the free end of the straw will point **down**. Unsettled weather with rain can be expected. Record barometer readings in your weather journal.

Anemometer: Arrange four plastic straws to form a cross. Tape the straws together at the center. Staple the top side of one Dixie cup to the end of each straw, or run each straw through the walls of a cup. Make sure the open ends of the cups all face the same direction. Push a straight pin through the center of the straws into the top of a pencil eraser. Place an X on one of the cups. This will be the cup you use for counting when the anemometer spins. Ten turns per minute means the wind speed is about one mile per hour. Record the wind speed in your weather journal.

Wind Speed: Wind speed is measured by using the Beaufort Wind Scale, which is a scale of 0–12 based on visual clues. The scale can be found at the following website. Print a copy of the scale for your weather station. "Beaufort Wind Scale." National Weather Association. <http://www.stormfax.com/beaufort.htm>

Section 1.3: Scientific Measurement Word List

The International System (SI) of Measurement
Scientists throughout the world use the SI system of measurement.

Measurement	Definition	SI Unit	Symbol
length	the distance between two points	meter	m
volume	the measure of the amount of space an object occupies	cubic meter	m^3
mass	the measure of the amount of matter in an object	kilogram	kg
weight	the measure of force	newton	N
temperature	the measure of the amount of heat an object has	kelvin	K
time	the measure for the interval between two events	second	s
area	the measure of the number of square units needed to cover the faces or surfaces of a figure	square meters	m^2

The Metric System is used to measure SI units.

Length	Mass	Capacity
1 centimeter (cm) = 10 millimeters (mm) 1 meter (m) = 100 cm 1 kilometer (km) = 1,000 m	1 kilogram (kg) = 1,000 grams (g)	1 liter (L) = 1,000 milliliters (mL)

Converting Metric Units

Rule: To change from large units of measurement to small units, multiply.

Example: *Try:*

Problem:	2 m = _____ cm		Problem:	5 m = _____ cm
Think:	1 m = 100 cm		Think:	1 m = 100 cm
Calculate:	2 x 100 = 200 cm		Calculate:	5 x 100 = _____ cm

Rule: To change from a small unit of measurement to a large unit, divide.

Example: *Try:*

Problem:	9 cm = _____ m		Problem:	2 cm = _____ m
Think:	100 cm = 1 m		Think:	100 cm = 1 m
Calculate:	9 ÷ 100 = 0.09 m		Calculate:	2 ÷ 100 = _____ m

Section 1.3: Scientific Measurement Word List (cont.)

Other Measurements Used in Science

Temperature is expressed in degrees (°). The Fahrenheit (°F) and Celsius (°C) temperature scales are the two most common scales used in science classrooms and on thermometers. Most thermometers have both scales. If you know the temperature in one scale, you can read across to tell the temperature in the other scale.

Reading a Thermometer:
Hold the thermometer at eye level. Do not put your fingers on the bulb of the thermometer.

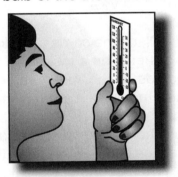

Measuring Temperature: Use these thermometers with the Fahrenheit and Celsius activity on page 15.

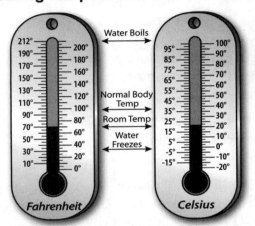

Time		
Conversion	**Unit**	**Abbreviation**
1 minute = 60 seconds	second	s
1 hour = 60 minutes	minute	min
1 day = 24 hours	hour	h
1 week = 7 days	day	d
4 weeks = 1 month (approx.)	week	wk
1 year = 12 months	month	mo
1 year = 52 weeks	year	y
1 year = 365 1/4 days		

Rule: To change from large units of measurement to small units, multiply.

Example: *Try:*

Problem:	2 h = _____ min		Problem:	4 h = _____ min
Think:	1 h = 60 min		Think:	1 h = 60 min
Calculate:	2 x 60 = 120 min		Calculate:	4 x 60 = _____ min

Rule: To change from a small unit of measurement to a large unit, divide.

Example: *Try:*

Problem:	14 d = _____ wk		Problem:	21 d = _____ wk
Think:	7 d = 1 wk		Think:	7 d = 1 wk
Calculate:	14 ÷ 7 = 2 wk		Calculate:	21 ÷ 7 = _____ wk

Section 1.3: Vocabulary Building Activities

Appropriate Units of Measurement:
Choose an appropriate unit to measure length: mm, cm, or m.

1. apple seed ___   3. earthworm ___
2. whale ___   4. flea ___

Choose an appropriate unit to measure mass: g or kg.

1. you ___   3. pine cone ___
2. dog ___   4. banana ___

Practice Measuring:
Have fun practicing reading length in centimeters at the two following websites.

1. "Measure It." Pearson Education, Inc. <http://www.funbrain.com/measure/>

2. "Length Strength: Centimeters." Harcourt School Publishers. <http://www.hbschool.com/activity/length_strength1_centi/>

Graduated Cylinder:
Practice measuring volume using a graduated cylinder. Place three graduated cylinders on a table. In one, pour 17 mL of liquid, in the next, pour 33 mL of liquid, and in the last, pour 61 mL liquid.

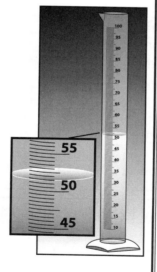

Reminder: When measuring liquid volume, you read the measurement from the bottom of the **meniscus**. The meniscus is the curve formed because of the adhesion of the liquid to the container.

Metric Match Up:
With a partner, write each of the following vocabulary words and abbreviations on separate index cards.

millimeter	mm	centimeter	cm
meter	m	kilometer	km
gram	g	kilogram	kg
milliliter	mL	liter	L
second	s	hour	h
day	d	week	w
month	mo	year	y

Shuffle the cards. Place the cards face down in 7 rows and 4 columns on a table. The first player picks 2 cards. If the measurements and abbreviations match, the player keeps the cards and picks 2 more. If the cards do not make a match, the player places the cards back on the table face down in the spots they were taken from. The second player takes a turn. The game continues until all the cards have been matched correctly. The player with the most matched cards wins the game.

Measuring Length:
With a partner, choose five objects in your classroom to measure. Estimate the length and then measure with a meter stick. Copy and complete the data table below in your science journal.

Object	Length	
	Estimate	Measurement
1.		
2.		
3.		
4.		
5.		

Section 1.3: Vocabulary Building Activities (cont.)

Fahrenheit and Celsius: Use the thermometers on page 13 to complete the data table below.

Item	°Fahrenheit	°Celsius
Water Boils		
Body Temperature		
Room Temperature		
Water Freezes		

Balance Scale: Fill different empty film canisters or pill bottles with various objects such as pennies, paper clips, popcorn, screws, or washers that will get you closest to the targeted mass. Now, measure the mass of each canister using a balance scale. Copy and complete the data table below in your science journal.

Target Mass	Items Used	Actual Mass
1 gram		
12 grams		
56 grams		

Thermometers: You can find out how hot or cold something is by measuring the temperature with a thermometer. Temperature is measured in both Celsius and Fahrenheit. With just a little practice, a thermometer is easy to read.

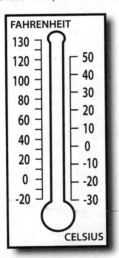

thermometer #1

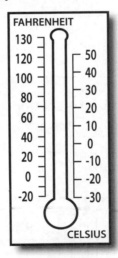

thermometer #2

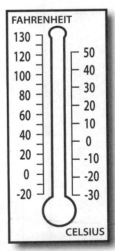

thermometer #3

1. Color in a mercury bar to 0 degrees Celsius on thermometer #1. Estimate the temperature in degrees Fahrenheit. _____

2. Color in a mercury bar to 72 degrees Fahrenheit on thermometer #2. Estimate the temperature in degrees Celsius. _____

3. Color in a mercury bar to 20 degrees Fahrenheit on thermometer #3. Estimate the temperature in degrees Celsius. _____

Section 2.1: Matter Word List

acid **as**-id ac·id	**definition:** a solution with a pH of less than 7 **context:** Vinegar is an **acid** and measures 4 on the pH scale.
atom **at**-əm at·om	**definition:** a small particle that makes up most kinds of matter **context: Atoms** are too small to see, so models are used to explain them.
base **bās** base	**definition:** a solution with a pH more than 7 **context:** Ammonia is a **base** and measures 11 on the pH scale.
chemical change **kem**-i-kəl **chānj** chem·i·cal change	**definition:** the change of a substance into a new substance with different properties **context:** Digesting food is an example of a **chemical change**.
chemical property **kem**-i-kəl **prop**-ər-tē chem·i·cal prop·er·ty	**definition:** a characteristic of a substance that allows it to change to a new substance **context:** A **chemical property** of iron is that when it reacts with oxygen in the air, it starts to rust.
compound **kom**-pound com·pound	**definition:** the new substance produced when two or more substances are chemically combined **context:** Water is a **compound** that contains hydrogen and oxygen.
density **den**-si-tē den·si·ty	**definition:** the amount of mass in a certain volume **context:** The **density** of ice is less than that of the soft drink, so ice floats in it.
electron i-**lek**-tron e·lec·tron	**definition:** an invisible, negatively charged particle that travels around the nucleus of an atom **context: Electrons** surround the nucleus of an atom.
element **el**-ə-mənt el·e·ment	**definition:** the simplest form of matter **context:** There are 111 named **elements**.
gas gas gas	**definition:** a substance that has no definite shape or volume **context:** Oxygen is a **gas** that can expand to fill the container in which it is held.
indicator **in**-di-kā-tər in·di·ca·tor	**definition:** a substance that changes color in acids or bases **context:** Litmus paper is an **indicator** used in determining the pH of a solution.
liquid **lik**-wid liq·uid	**definition:** a substance with a definite volume but no definite shape **context:** Water is a **liquid** that keeps the same volume but changes shape when placed in a different container.
mass mas mass	**definition:** the amount of matter in objects and substances **context:** The **mass** of a whale is greater than the mass of a trout.

Section 2.1: Matter Word List (cont.)

matter mat-ər mat·ter	**definition:** the term used to describe anything that has mass and takes up space **context:** Everything in the universe is made of **matter**.
mixture miks-chər mix·ture	**definition:** the substance formed when two or more substances come together but do not combine to make a new substance **context:** A fruit salad is an example of a **mixture**.
neutral no͞o-trəl neu·tral	**definition:** a solution measuring 7 on the pH scale **context:** Distilled water is a **neutral** solution and measures 7 on the pH scale.
neutron no͞o-tron neu·tron	**definition:** an uncharged particle located in the nucleus of an atom **context:** **Neutrons**, which have no charge, are in the nucleus of an atom.
nucleus no͞o-klē-əs nu·cle·us	**definition:** the positively charged, central part of an atom **context:** The protons and neutrons are found in the **nucleus** of an atom.
periodic table pir-ē-od-ik tā-bəl per·i·od·ic ta·ble	**definition:** a chart that organizes the elements by the number of protons in each element's nucleus **context:** A **periodic table** contains data about the elements.
pH pē-āch p·H	**definition:** a measure of how acidic or basic a solution is, the scale ranges from 0–14 **context:** Vinegar is an acid and measures 4 on the **pH** scale.
physical change fiz-i-kəl chānj phys·i·cal change	**definition:** a change in size, shape, or form of matter **context:** Ice melting is a **physical change**.
physical property fiz-i-kəl prop-ər-tē phys·i·cal prop·er·ty	**definition:** a characteristic of matter that can be observed, such as color, size, shape, taste, texture, and form **context:** All matter has **physical properties**.
proton prō-ton pro·ton	**definition:** a positively charged particle located in the nucleus of an atom **context:** **Protons** and neutrons are in the nucleus of an atom.
solid sol-id sol·id	**definition:** a substance that has a definite shape and volume **context:** A brick is an example of a **solid**.
state of matter stāt uv mat-ər state of mat·ter	**definition:** a physical property of matter: solid, liquid, and gas **context:** **State of matter** is a physical property.
substance sub-stəns sub·stance	**definition:** matter with a fixed composition whose identity can be changed by chemical processes but not by ordinary physical processes **context:** A bar of gold is an example of a **substance**.
volume vol-yo͞om vol·ume	**definition:** the measure of how much space an object or substance takes up **context:** A graduated cylinder is used to measure **volume**.

Section 2.1: Vocabulary Building Activities

Physical vs. Chemical Changes: Decide whether the changes listed below are chemical or physical. Record the answers in your science journal.

1. freezing water
2. rotting wood
3. cake baking
4. burning paper
5. bread molding
6. shredding paper
7. crushing rock
8. drying clothes
9. folding paper
10. iron rusting
11. ice melting
12. bouncing ball

pH Scale: A pH scale is a device that helps measure how acidic or basic a solution is. The scale ranges from 0 to 14: pH of 7 is neutral, pH below 7 is acidic (acid), and pH above 7 is alkaline (base).

Step 1: Copy the pH Scale below in your science journal.

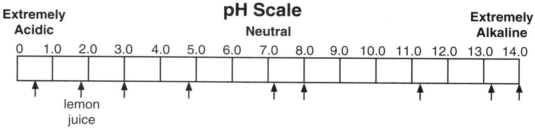

Step 2: Place the names of the substances listed in the pH Values of Common Substances Table below under the correct value on your pH scale. Lemon juice has been added to the scale for you.

Step 3: Copy the pH Values of Common Substances Table below in your science journal. Complete the table by identifying each substance as acid, base, or neutral. Bleach has been done for you.

pH Values of Common Substances Table				
Substance	pH Level	Acid	Base (alkaline)	Neutral
1. lemon juice	1.8			
2. sea water	8.0			
3. bleach	13.2		X	
4. battery acid	0.5			
5. orange juice	4.8			
6. ammonia	11.2			
7. vinegar	3.0			
8. lye	14.0			
9. bood	7.2			

Section 2.1: Vocabulary Building Activities (cont.)

Online Resource: Learn about the parts of an atom at the following interactive website. "Atom Builder." Public Broadcasting Service. <http://www.pbs.org/wgbh/aso/tryit/atom/#>

Mixtures vs. Compounds: Explain the difference between mixtures and compounds, and give an example of both in your science journal.

Identify Physical Properties: Physical properties of matter are characteristics that can be observed, such as color, shape, smell, taste, and texture. Copy the data table below in your science journal. Observe five objects in the classroom and complete the table.

Object	Color	Texture	Shape	Smell	Taste
1.					
2.					
3.					
4.					
5.					

Vocabulary Code Puzzle: Decode the physical science vocabulary words using the code below.

a	b	c	d	e	f	g	h	i	j	k	l	m	n	o	p	q	r	s	t	u	v	w	x	y	z
13	4	20	1	11	2	16	5	18	3	22	8	19	26	17	21	6	24	10	9	25	15	23	7	12	14

1. 15-17-8-25-19-11 _____

2. 16-13-10 _____

3. 11-8-11-19-11-26-9 _____

4. 8-18-6-25-18-1 _____

5. 1-11-26-10-18-9-12 _____

Create your own alphabet code puzzle. Code five matter vocabulary words. Trade your puzzle with a partner. Try solving the new decoding puzzle.

States of Matter: There are three states of matter: solid, liquid, and gas. Copy the table below in your science journal. Study the pictures and descriptions. Write the names of each picture under the correct heading on your table.

 ice air  water fish  milk exhaust

Solids	Liquids	Gases
_____	_____	_____
_____	_____	_____

Section 2.2: Energy Word List

absorption əb-**sôrp**-shən ab·sorp·tion	**definition:** the transfer of radiant energy into a different form usually causing a rise in temperature **context: Absorption** of the sun's rays warms the earth.
circuit **sûr**-kit cir·cuit	**definition:** a continuous path of flowing electrons from a source, through wires, and back to the source **context:** A **circuit** carries electrical energy to a device.
conductor kən-**duk**-tər con·duc·tor	**definition:** a material that allows electrons to move or that transfers heat easily **context:** Copper is a good **conductor** of electricity.
crest **krest** crest	**definition:** the high point of a wave **context:** Troughs are the low points of waves, and **crests** are the high points.
current **kûr**-ənt cur·rent	**definition:** the rate of flow of electric charge past a given point in an electric circuit **context:** Electric **current** moves in a confined path.
electrical energy i-**lek**-tri-kəl **en**-ər-jē e·lec·tri·cal en·er·gy	**definition:** the energy carried by electric current **context:** Lightbulbs are powered by **electrical energy**.
electricity i-lek-**tris**-ə-tē e·lec·tric·i·ty	**definition:** the interaction between electric charges **context:** Benjamin Franklin experimented with **electricity** in the 1700s.
electromagnet i-lek-trō-**mag**-nit e·lec·tro·mag·net	**definition:** a magnet made by wrapping a current-carrying wire around an iron core **context:** An **electromagnet** is responsible for making an electric doorbell ring.
energy **en**-ər-jē en·er·gy	**definition:** the ability to cause change **context:** When dribbling a ball down a basketball court, you are using **energy**.
heat **hēt** heat	**definition:** the transfer of energy from one object to another **context:** When **heat** is added to an object, the temperature rises.
heat transfer **hēt** trans-**fûr** heat trans·fer	**definition:** the flow of heat from one object to another **context:** Conduction, radiation, and convection are the three ways that **heat transfer** occurs.
insulator in-sə-**lā**-tər in·su·la·tor	**definition:** a material in which electrons have restricted movement **context:** Rubber and plastic are examples of **insulators** that do not conduct electricity well.
light energy **līt en**-ər-jē light en·er·gy	**definition:** the sun's rays **context: Light energy** can be absorbed, reflected, or transmitted.
magnet **mag**-nit mag·net	**definition:** a device used to attract or repel other objects made of iron or steel **context:** A rock containing the mineral magnetite acts as a **magnet**.

Section 2.2: Energy Word List (cont.)

magnetic field mag-**net**-ik fēld mag·net·ic field	**definition:** an area that surrounds a magnet where a magnetic force can be detected **context:** All magnets are surrounded by a **magnetic field**.
mechanical energy mi-**kan**-i-kəl **en**-ər-jē me·chan·i·cal en·er·gy	**definition:** the total kinetic and potential energy of an object **context:** Car engines convert thermal energy into **mechanical energy**.
poles **pōlz** poles	**definition:** the points in a magnetized body where magnetism is stronger **context:** All magnets have a north **pole** and a south **pole**.
reflection ri-**flek**-shən re·flec·tion	**definition:** the light energy bouncing off an object or surface **context:** Seeing yourself in a mirror is an example of light **reflection**.
refraction ri-**frak**-shən re·frac·tion	**definition:** the light energy bending as it moves from one medium into another medium **context:** Objects appear closer underwater and may be hard to grasp because of **refraction**.
sound **sound** sound	**definition:** the energy transferred by an object vibrating in the air **context:** Some medical problems can be treated using **sound** waves.
static electricity **stat**-ik i-lek-**tris**-ə-tē stat·ic e·lec·tric·i·ty	**definition:** a buildup of charges on an object **context:** Lightning is a discharge of **static electricity**.
temperature **tem**-pər-ə-cho͞or tem·per·a·ture	**definition:** a measurement of the amount of heat an object contains **context:** After sitting in the sun, the **temperature** of the car was 190° F.
thermal energy **thûr**-məl **en**-ər-jē ther·mal en·er·gy	**definition:** the sum of the kinetic and potential energy of the particles in a material **context:** Hot coffee has **thermal energy** that moves from the cup to the cool air around it.
transmission trans-**mish**-ən trans·mis·sion	**definition:** the traveling of radio waves in the space between transmitting and receiving radio or television stations **context:** The radio **transmission** went out from the antenna in all directions.
trough **trof** trough	**definition:** the low point on a wave **context:** Crests are the high points of waves, and **troughs** are the low points.
wave **wāv** wave	**definition:** a disturbance that carries energy from point to point with a rhythm **context:** A sound **wave** made by a clap of thunder carries a large amount of energy.

Section 2.2: Vocabulary Building Activities

Heat Transfer: Heat is the transfer of thermal energy between substances that are at different temperatures. The three methods of heat transfer are conduction, convection, and radiation. Copy and complete the data table below in your science journal.

Example	Method of Transfer
1.　sun heating the earth	
2.　spoon becomes warm in a cup of hot soup	
3.　heating a pot of water on the stove	

Forms of Energy: Energy is a property of matter. There are many different forms of energy including mechanical, thermal, light, sound, and electrical. Copy and complete the data table below in your science journal.

	Example	Form of Energy
1.	lightbulb is lit	
2.	pot of boiling water	
3.	a band playing	
4.	book falls off a table	
5.	car traveling down the street	

Magnetic Field: A magnetic field is the region around a magnet that is affected by magnetic force. Iron filings can be used to show the lines of magnetic force.

1. Place a bar magnet on a sheet of white paper. Sprinkle iron filings on the paper. Draw the lines of force on the magnet below.

S		N

2. Place two bar magnets on a sheet of white paper with similar poles toward each other. Sprinkle iron filings on the paper. Draw the lines of force on the magnets below.

S	N		N	S

3. Place two bar magnets on a sheet of white paper with a north pole and a south pole toward each other. Draw the lines of force on the magnets below.

S	N		S	N

Light: When light traveling through the air strikes a different medium such as water or glass, it suddenly changes direction and "bends." Raindrops and prisms separate white light into the colors of the spectrum. Look through a prism. Record the answers to the questions below in your science journal.

1. What happened when you viewed white light through the prism?
2. What colors did you see?
3. In what order were the colors?

Magnet: What can a magnet pick up? Find eight objects in your classroom. Write them in a data table in your science journal. Test each object with a magnet to see if the magnet can pick it up or not. Record the results in the table.

Section 2.2: Vocabulary Building Activities (cont.)

Mechanical Energy: There are two kinds of mechanical energy—kinetic and potential. Kinetic energy is the energy an object has because it is moving. Potential energy is stored energy. Copy the data table below in your science journal. Classify each example as kinetic or potential energy.

Example	Energy
1. a ball bouncing	
2. a rocket on a launch pad	
3. a can of gasoline	
4. a flashlight turned off	
5. car moving down the street	

Insulator or Conductor?: Certain materials are able to carry an electric current. These materials are called conductors. Other materials are not good at carrying current. These materials are called insulators. Copy and complete the data table in your science journal. Classify each object as conductor or insulator.

Object	Conductor or Insulator?
1. plastic	
2. copper	
3. glass	
4. paper	
5. key	
6. paper clip	
7. rock	

Online Resource: Learn more about electricity at the following interactive website. "Electricity." Woodlands Junior School. <http://www.woodlands-junior.kent.sch.uk/revision/Science/electricity.htm>

Sound: Sounds are vibrations in the form of waves. Tape a 25-cm length of string to a ping-pong ball. Grasp the end of the string and hold it out in front of you so that the ping-pong ball hangs down. Strike a tuning fork and place it next to the ping-pong ball so that it barely touches. Record your observations in your science journal. Explain what happened.

Circuits: Electric current flows through a path called a circuit. Look at each diagram below. Using a flashlight blub, insulated wire, and a D-cell battery, try to light the bulb in the way shown in each picture. Can you make the bulb light? Record the answers in your science journal.

1. yes/no   2. yes/no   3. yes/no   4. yes/no   5. yes/no   6. yes/no

Section 2.3: Force and Motion Word List

acceleration ak-sel-ə-**rā**-shən ac·cel·e·ra·tion	**definition:** the change in an object's speed or direction over time **context:** If an object speeds up, the **acceleration** is in the direction that the object is moving.
buoyancy **boi**-ən-sē buoy·an·cy	**definition:** an object's ability to float **context:** Icebergs floating in the ocean demonstrate the power of **buoyancy**.
compound machine **kom**-pound mə-**shēn** com·pound ma·chine	**definition:** a machine made from two or more simple machines **context:** A bicycle is a **compound machine**.
electric force i-**lek**-trik **fôrs** e·lec·tric force	**definition:** an attractive or repulsive force between electrically charged objects **context: Electric force** gets stronger as the objects get closer.
force **fôrs** force	**definition:** a push or a pull **context:** A **force** is applied to a desk to push it across the room.
free fall **frē fôl** free fall	**definition:** the movement of a falling object when the only force acting on it is gravity **context:** Regardless of mass, all objects in **free fall** accelerate at the same rate.
friction **frik**-shən fric·tion	**definition:** a force that acts to oppose sliding between two surfaces that are touching **context:** Rubbing your hands together creates **friction**.
gravity **grav**-i-tē grav·i·ty	**definition:** the force that pulls objects toward each other **context:** The force of **gravity** gives you weight.
inclined plane in-**klīnd plān** in·clined plane	**definition:** a simple machine that is a flat, sloping surface over which objects can be moved to a higher level **context:** A ramp is an **inclined plane**.
inertia in-**ûr**-shə in·er·tia	**definition:** an object's tendency to resist a change of motion **context:** The more mass an object has, the more **inertia** it has.
lever **lev**-ər lev·er	**definition:** a simple machine having a rod that rotates about a point called a fulcrum **context:** Opening a paint can is easy with a **lever**.
lift **lift** lift	**definition:** an upward force **context:** Large-winged planes provide more **lift** to carry heavy loads.
magnetic force mag-**net**-ik **fôrs** mag·net·ic force	**definition:** a force produced by interacting magnetic poles **context: Magnetic forces** lift and propel the maglev train.

Section 2.3: Force and Motion Word List (cont.)

mass mas mass	**definition:** the amount of matter in an object **context:** An object's **mass** is always the same, but an object's weight depends on gravity.
momentum mō-men-təm mo·men·tum	**definition:** a measure of how hard it is to stop a moving object **context:** A seatbelt stops your **momentum** in a car.
motion mō-shən mo·tion	**definition:** an act in which one object's distance from another is changing **context:** You are in **motion** while running a race.
Newton's Laws of Motion nōōt-ns lôz uv mō-shən New·tons Laws of Mo·tion	**definition:** the rules and formulas for force, motion, acceleration, and mass **context: Newton's Laws of Motion** explain force, motion, acceleration, and mass.
pressure presh-ər pres·sure	**definition:** the amount of force exerted on a surface divided by the area **context:** The formula for **pressure** is force divided by area.
pulley pōōl-ē pul·ley	**definition:** a simple machine that has a grooved wheel with a cable wrapped over it **context:** There are two types of **pulleys**, fixed and movable.
screw skrōō screw	**definition:** a simple machine that is an inclined plane wrapped around a cylinder to form a spiral **context:** The tighter the threads of a **screw**, the easier it is to turn.
simple machine sim-pəl mə-shēn sim·ple ma·chine	**definition:** a machine that changes the amount, distance, or direction of a force needed to do work **context:** Inclined plane, wedge, screw, lever, wheel and axle, and pulley are the six kinds of **simple machines**.
speed spēd speed	**definition:** the distance traveled divided by the time it takes to travel that distance **context:** A wave moving through water moves at a different **speed** than a wave moving through air.
wedge wej wedge	**definition:** a simple machine that has two inclined planes back to back **context:** An ax head is an example of a **wedge**.
weight wāt weight	**definition:** a measurement of the amount of gravitational pull on an object exerted by the force of gravity on its mass **context: Weight** equals mass times force of gravity.
wheel and axle hwēl ənd ak-səl wheel and ax·le	**definition:** a simple machine consisting of two attached circular objects of different sizes that rotate together **context:** A ferris wheel and door knob are two devices that use a **wheel and axle**.
work wûrk work	**definition:** a force applied to an object, and the object moves as a result of the force **context:** Riding a bicycle to school is an example of **work**.

Section 2.3: Vocabulary Building Activities

Machines: A simple machine is a device that makes work easier. There are six simple machines. Look at each picture below and identify the simple machine. Record the answers in your science journal.

1.

2.

3.

4.

5.

6.

Online Resource: Learn more about simple machines at the following interactive website. "Simple Machines." COSI/Columbus. <http://www.cosi.org/files/Flash/simpMach/sm1.swf>

Resistance to Motion: Friction is a force that slows down and stops moving objects. It is a resistance to motion. Friction is created whenever objects rub against each other. Friction can produce heat and wear objects down. Complete the two activities below. Record the answers to the questions in your science journal.

Activity #1: Rub the palms of your hands together quickly for 30 seconds. What did you feel?

Activity #2: Put a few drops of liquid dishwashing soap on your hands. Rub your hands together quickly for 30 seconds. Did your hands feel the same as they did without the soap? Why?

How did using dishwashing soap help reduce the friction between your hands?

Lift: Because of the unique shape of the wing of an airplane, the air flowing over the top of the wing moves faster than air flowing under the wing. This causes an upward push on the wing. This upward force is called lift. Try the following activity to see how lift works.

Activity: Cut a strip of paper nine inches long and two inches wide. Hold it by the narrow end and blow across the upper surface of the paper. What happened to the paper? Explain how lift plays a role in helping birds fly. Record the answer in your science journal.

Section 2.3: Vocabulary Building Activities (cont.)

Compound Machines: Find five compound machines. Copy the data table below in your science journal. Be sure to leave plenty of room for listing the simple machines and the descriptions. Carefully examine each compound machine and complete the table. List the simple machines found in the compound machine. Describe how the simple machines identified in each compound machine work together to perform a task.

Compound Machine	Simple Machines in the Compound Machine	Description
1.		
2.		
3.		
4.		
5.		

Magnetic Force: Magnetic force can be measured. Find the distance a bar magnet can move a paper clip. Place a paper clip on a table. Lay a plastic or wooden centimeter ruler down beside the paper clip. Slowly slide the magnet along the edge of the ruler, toward the paper clip. When the paper clip starts to move toward the magnet, measure how far it is between the magnet and the paper clip. Copy the data table below in your science journal. Record your measurements in the table. Repeat the activity three times.

Trials	Length
Trial #1	
Trial #2	
Trial #3	

Venn Diagram: Compare and contrast mass and weight. Copy an enlarged version of the Venn diagram in your science journal and complete the comparison of mass and weight.

Mass   Weight

Float or Sink?: Buoyancy is the force that makes an object float. With a partner, experiment with foil to create two shapes that will float. Sketch the boats in your science journals. Predict which boat will sink first when pennies are added. Carefully float the foil boats in a container of water. Gently add one penny at a time to each boat. Keep adding pennies until the boats sink. Count how many pennies each boat could support before sinking (the penny that sank the boat does not count). Record the number in your science journal.

Word Scramblers: Use the vocabulary list to help you unscramble the words below. Write the answers in your science journal.

1. n t i i o r c f _ _ _ _ _ _ _ _
2. u y n o b y c a _ _ _ _ _ _ _ _
3. l l p y u e _ _ _ _ _ _
4. s m a s _ _ _ _
5. t i i a e n r _ _ _ _ _ _ _

Create five more word scramblers. Trade with a partner and try to solve the new word scramblers.

Section 3.1: Cells Word List

cell sel cell	**definition:** the smallest living thing **context:** All organisms are made up of one or more **cells**.
cell membrane sel mem-brān cell mem·brane	**definition:** a thin layer that encloses the cell and controls what enters and leaves the cell **context:** Tiny pores in the **cell membrane** allow food, water, and oxygen to pass into the cell and waste to pass out of the cell.
cell wall sel wôl cell wall	**definition:** a structure that surrounds the cell membrane in plants; provides shape and support **context:** The **cell wall** is a stiff protective layer around the cell membrane of plant cells.
chlorophyll klôr-ə-fil chlor·o·phyll	**definition:** a green chemical in plant cells that allows plants to use the sun's energy for making food **context:** **Chlorophyll** is the green chemical in plant cells that helps them make their own food.
chloroplast klôr-ə-plast chlor·o·plast	**definition:** a disc-shaped organelle in plant cells; contains chlorophyll that helps plants make food and gives them their green color **context:** **Chloroplasts** are the food-making structures of the plant cell.
chromosome krō-mə-sōm chro·mo·some	**definition:** the structure in the nucleus that contains the genetic information that directs cell activity **context:** Humans have 23 pairs of **chromosomes**.
cytoplasm sī-tə-plaz-əm cy·to·plas·m	**definition:** a gel-like material that contains proteins, nutrients, and all of the other cell organelles **context:** The **cytoplasm** is where the food, water, and oxygen taken in by the cell are used.
deoxyribonucleic acid dē-ok-sē-**rī**-bō-noo-klē-ik **as**-id de·ox·y·ri·bo·nu·cle·ic ac·id	**definition:** the genetic information of the cell **context:** The traits that make organisms different from one another are contained in the DNA (**deoxyribonucleic acid**).
diffusion di-**fyoo**-zhən dif·fu·sion	**definition:** the movement of molecules into and out of the cell **context:** The process of **diffusion** helps the cell carry out all the basic life activities.
endoplasmic reticulum en-də-plaz-mik ri-**tik**-yə-ləm en·do·plas·mic re·tic·u·lum	**definition:** the transportation system for the cell **context:** The **endoplasmic reticulum** is the transportation system for the cell.
eukaryotic cell yoo-kar-ē-**ot**-ik sel eu·kar·y·ot·ic cell	**definition:** a single cell with a nucleus **context:** All organisms except bacteria are made up of **eukaryotic cells**.
Golgi body gôl-jē **bod**-ē Gol·gi bod·y	**definition:** a structure that packages and distributes protein outside the cell **context:** The **Golgi body** is responsible for packaging proteins for the cell.

Section 3.1: Cells Word List (cont.)

Hooke, Robert **Rob**-ərt **Hŏŏk** Rob·ert Hooke	**definition:** the first scientist to see cells with a microscope **context:** In 1655, **Robert Hooke** observed cork tree cells using a primitive microscope.
Leeuwenhoek, Anton van an-tōn van **lā**-vən-hŭk An·ton van Leeu·wen·hoek	**definition:** the first scientist to observe living cells **context:** In 1674, **Anton van Leeuwenhoek** studied pond water and observed single-celled organisms.
mitochondria mī-tə-**kon**-drē-ə mi·to·chon·dri·a	**definition:** organelles that provide the cell with energy **context:** The **mitochondria** are called the "power house" of the cell because they provide the cell with energy.
molecule **mol**-i-kyōol mol·e·cule	**definition:** the smallest particle of a substance **context:** **Molecules** can go in and out of the cell by moving through the tiny holes in the cell membrane.
multicellular mul-ti-**sel**-yə-lər mul·ti·cell·u·lar	**definition:** an organism made up of many cells **context:** Snails, fish, trees, and humans are **multicellular**.
nuclear membrane nōō-klē-ər **mem**-brān nu·cle·ar mem·brane	**definition:** the membrane that surrounds the nucleus **context:** The **nuclear membrane** is often referred to as the nuclear envelope because it envelops the nucleus.
nucleus nōō-klē-əs nu·cle·us	**definition:** the control center for the cell **context:** The **nucleus** is usually located near the center of the cell and controls the activity of the cell.
organelle ôr-gə-**nel** or·ga·nelle	**definition:** one of the many tiny structures in the cytoplasm; each does a specific job for the cell **context:** **Organelles** are scattered throughout the cytoplasm.
organism **ôr**-gə-niz-əm or·ga·nis·m	**definition:** a living system capable of reproduction, growth, and maintenance **context:** In biology, an **organism** is a living system, such as an animal, plant, or microorganism.
osmosis oz-**mō**-sis os·mo·sis	**definition:** the movement of water molecules into and out of cells **context:** **Osmosis** is the process that allows water molecules to move into and out of a cell.
prokaryotic cell prō-kar-ē-**ot**-ik **sel** pro·kar·y·ot·ic cell	**definition:** the simplest type of cell; cell has no nucleus; DNA and other materials float "freely" inside the cytoplasm **context:** Bacteria are a good example of **prokaryotic cells**.
ribosome **rī**-bə-sōm ri·bo·some	**definition:** an organelle that makes protein for the cell **context:** A **ribosome** makes proteins that will be used inside a cell.
unicellular yōō-ni-**sel**-yə-lər u·ni·cel·lu·lar	**definition:** an organism made up of only one cell **context:** Many organisms, including bacteria, are **unicellular**.
vacuole **vak**-yōō-ōl vac·u·ole	**definition:** a structure that stores food, water, and waste for the cell **context:** Plant cells often have only one large **vacuole**.

Section 3.1: Vocabulary Building Activities

Three Main Parts of a Cell: All eukaryotic cells have three things in common. They all have a cell membrane, nucleus, and cytoplasm. Identify the cell parts in the diagram below. Record the answers in your science journal.

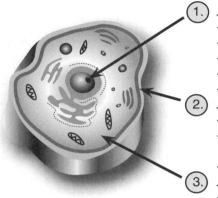

1. _____
   - controls all the cell activities
   - round or egg-shaped structure
   - found near the center of the cell
   - dark in color
   - contains DNA

2. _____
   - thin layer that encloses the cell
   - controls movement of material into and out of cell
   - offers shape and protection for cell

3. _____
   - gel-like material
   - contains proteins, nutrients, and all the other cell organelles

Animal Cell

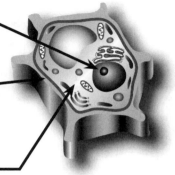

Plant Cell

Cell Review: Write the letter of the correct answer for each item on the line provided. Then record the answers in your science journal.

1. All living things are made up of ____.
   a. many cells   b. one or more cells

2. Substances move in and out of a cell by a process called ____.
   a. photosynthesis   b. diffusion

3. Structures within the cell are called ____.
   a. organelles   b. osmosis

Online Resources: Practice identifying the parts of a plant and animal cell at the following interactive website.

"Cells alive." James L. Sullivan. 2006. Quill Graphics. <http://www.cellsalive/>

Cell Bingo: With a partner, practice the vocabulary from the cell word list. Fold a sheet of white paper into four vertical columns. Unfold the paper. Now fold the paper into four horizontal rows. Unfold the paper. Write "Free" in one of the squares. Fill in the remaining squares with vocabulary words. The caller reads a definition. The player searches for the matching vocabulary word on the bingo sheet. When the player finds a match, a bean is placed on the square. When the player has filled in the squares in a diagonal, vertical, or horizontal pattern on the card, the player yells, "Bingo!"

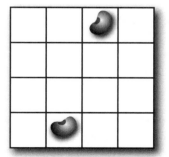

Section 3.1: Vocabulary Building Activities (cont.)

Venn Diagram: Compare and contrast the structure of a plant and animal cell. Complete the Venn diagram below, or copy and complete the Venn diagram in your science journal.

Plant and Animal Cell Venn Diagram

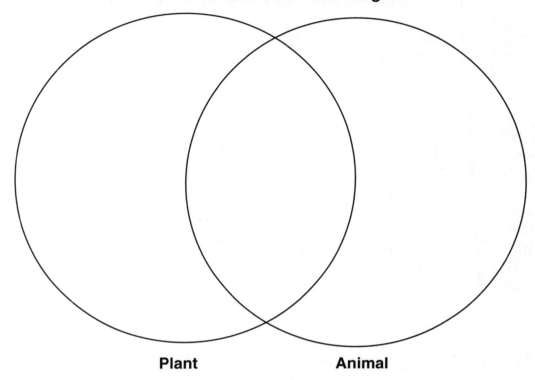

Plant   Animal

Why do plant cells have a cell wall and animal cells do not? _____

_____

Organisms: All organisms are made up of cells. Some living things are unicellular and carry out all the basic life activities within that single cell. However, most living things are multicellular. Copy and complete the table below with definitions and examples in your science journal.

Organism	Definition	Example
unicellular		
multicelluar		

Animal Cell Model: Pour white corn syrup into a resealable baggie. Then, put that baggie into a second one for extra strength. Decide which objects might best represent the organelles in a cell and add them to the interior baggie. Seal both bags. Objects to represent organelles could include a variety of candies, cereal, gummi worms, mints, gum balls, rope licorice, jelly beans, and other candies. Create a key for your cell model.

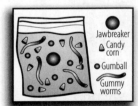

Section 3.2: Plants Word List

carbon dioxide kär-bən dī-**ok**-sīd car·bon di·ox·ide	**definition:** a gas that animals release back into the environment as waste and plants take in during the process of photosynthesis **context:** During photosynthesis, plants take in **carbon dioxide** through the stomata in the leaf.
chlorophyll **klôr**-ə-fil chlor·o·phyll	**definition:** a green chemical in plant cells that allows plants to use the sun's energy for making food **context: Chlorophyll** is the green chemical in plant cells that helps them make their own food.
cone **kōn** cone	**definition:** a seed-bearing organ covered with woody scales on conifer plants **context:** Seeds can be found in the **cones** of a pine tree.
coniferous tree kō-**nif**-ər-əs **trē** co·nif·er·ous tree	**definition:** a tree with needle-like leaves that produces seeds in cones **context:** Pine trees are **coniferous trees**.
cotyledon kot-ə-**lē**-dən cot·y·le·don	**definition:** the leaf or leaves developed by the embryo of a plant seed **context:** Monocot plants have one **cotyledon** or seed leaf.
deciduous tree di-**sij**-o͞o-əs **trē** de·cid·u·ous tree	**definition:** a tree that loses its leaves in the winter **context:** Maple, oak, and walnut trees are just a few of the **deciduous trees**.
dicot **dī**-kot di·cot	**definition:** a plant with two cotyledons in each seed **context: Dicot** (dicotyledon) plants like soybeans have flowers with four or five petals.
flower **flou**-ər flow·er	**definition:** the plant part that performs the job of reproduction **context:** The **flower** is the reproductive structure found in flowering plants.
germination jûr-mə-**nā**-shən ger·mi·na·tion	**definition:** the time it takes for a seed to sprout **context:** Seed **germination** depends on three factors: temperature, moisture, and air.
glucose **glo͞o**-kōs glu·cose	**definition:** the sugar produced in the leaf of a plant during photosynthesis **context: Glucose** is the food produced during photosynthesis.
leaf **lēf** leaf	**definition:** a green, flat outgrowth from a plant stem used to make food **context:** Photosynthesis takes place in the plant **leaf**.
monocot **mon**-ə-kot mon·o·cot	**definition:** a plant with one cotyledon in each seed **context: Monocot** (monocotyledon) plants like lillies have flowers with petals of three or multiples of three.
oxygen **ok**-si-jən ox·y·gen	**definition:** a gas that animals need and plants release during the process of photosynthesis **context:** During photosynthesis, **oxygen** is released back into the environment as a waste product.

Section 3.2: Plants Word List (cont.)

phloem **flō**-em phlo·em	**definition:** the tissue through which food from the leaves moves down through the rest of a plant **context: Phloem** tissue transports sugar made in the leaves to other parts of the plant.
photosynthesis fō-tō-**sin**-thi-sis pho·to·syn·the·sis	**definition:** the food-making process in green plants that uses sunlight **context:** During **photosynthesis**, carbon dioxide, sunlight, and water combine with chlorophyll to produce glucose.
pistil **pis**-tl pis·til	**definition:** the female reproductive part of the flower **context:** The **pistil** consists of the stigma, style, ovary, and egg cells.
plant **plant** plant	**definition:** a multicellular organism that makes its own food in a process called photosynthesis **context: Plants** that contain chlorophyll can make their own food.
pollen **pol**-ən pol·len	**definition:** a plant sperm cell **context:** The movement of **pollen** from the anther to the stigma is necessary for seeds to form in flowering plants.
pollination pol-ə-**nā**-shən pol·li·na·tion	**definition:** the transfer of a pollen grain to the egg-producing part of a plant **context:** Some flowering plants depend on the wind for **pollination**.
root **rōot** root	**definition:** the underground part of a plant that anchors the plant and stores extra food **context:** The **root** of a plant absorbs water from the soil.
seed **sēd** seed	**definition:** an undeveloped plant with stored food sealed in a protective covering **context:** A seed has three parts: seed coat, cotyledon, and embryo.
spore **spôr** spore	**definition:** a reproductive cell of a non-flowering plant **context: Spores** of a fern are easily spread by the wind.
stamen **stā**-mən sta·men	**definition:** the male reproductive part of a flower **context:** The **stamen** contains the anther, filament, and pollen.
stem **stem** stem	**definition:** the above-ground support system of a plant that holds the leaves up to the light **context:** The **stem** of a plant transports water from the roots and food from the leaves to other parts of the plant.
stomata **stō**-mə-tə sto·ma·ta	**definition:** tiny opening in the leaf **context:** Plants take in carbon dioxide and release oxygen through the **stomata** during photosynthesis.
xylem **zī**-ləm xy·lem	**definition:** the tissue through which water and minerals move up through a plant **context:** Vascular plants contain **xylem** tissue.

Section 3.2: Vocabulary Building Activities

Leaves: Leaves have the same basic parts, but they are not all put together in the same way. Copy each of the data tables in your science journal. Complete the tables by drawing an example of each type of leaf.

Type of Leaf	Examples
simple leaf	
compound leaf	

Leaf Veins	Examples
parallel veins	
net-veined leaves	

Leaf Food Factory: Photosynthesis (process plants use to make food) happens in the leaf. The green leaves absorb light energy from the sun. They also take in carbon dioxide from the air through the **stomata** (openings) in the leaf. Water and minerals from the soil travel through the roots and stems of the plant to mix with chlorophyll, sunlight, and carbon dioxide to produce **glucose** (sugar). Draw a  diagram explaining the process of photosynthesis in your science journal.

Leaf Collection: Create a leaf book. Collect examples of simple and compound leaves, parallel and netted veined leaves, and different types of leaf attachments. Place each leaf sample between sheets of newspaper. Place the leaves in between the pages of a telephone book. After several days, take leaves out of the telephone book and separate them from the newspaper. The leaves will be flat and dry. Place each leaf sample between two sheets of wax paper. Then place the leaf and wax paper between the newspapers. Press the paper with a very warm iron. This will seal the leaf between the wax paper. Glue the sealed leaves to white construction paper and label. Design a cover for the leaf book, add the leaf pages, and staple.

Seed Germination: Place a paper towel around the inside of two jars. Place four seeds (bean, radish, or lettuce) between the paper towel and the side of each jar. Moisten the paper towel in one jar. Leave the paper towel dry in the other jar. Place the jars in a warm, sunny location. Keep paper towels in the one jar moist. Record the changes in the seeds in your science journal. What is the job of water in germination?

Sunlight and Photosynthesis: Cover one leaf of a geranium plant with aluminum foil. Set the plant in a sunny place. Water the plant when needed. After a week, remove the aluminum foil from the leaf. Record observations in your science journal. Why was covering the leaf with foil harmful to the plant? Record the answer in your science journal.

Chlorophyll: Place green leaves in a beaker. Add enough rubbing alcohol to the beaker to cover the leaves. Place the beaker in hot water and let sit for 30 minutes. Replace hot water if needed. Remove the beaker from the water. Record observations in your science journal.

1. Why does the alcohol turn green?
2. Why do leaves turn colors in the fall?

Word Search: Create your own word search puzzle using 12 vocabulary words from this section. Trade with a partner and try the word searches.

Section 3.2: Vocabulary Building Activities (cont.)

Parts of a Plant: Most plants have three main parts. Copy and complete the data table in your science journal.

Plant Part	Function
Root	
Stem	
Leaf	

Deciduous and Coniferous Trees: Make a folder book. Hold a sheet of construction paper horizontally and fold it in half. Unfold the paper. Fold the bottom edge of the paper up to form a two-inch pocket and staple each side. Label one side of the folder "Coniferous Trees" and the other side "Deciduous Trees." Using magazines and seed catalogs, cut out pictures of trees and place them in the correct pocket of the folder.

Plant Roots: Make root-viewing boxes using clean, empty milk cartons. Cut away one side of the carton. Insert a plastic sandwich bag into the milk carton and fill it with soil. Soak a variety of seeds overnight and then plant the seeds in the viewing boxes. Place the boxes in a sunny place, keeping the soil moist. Observe growth of the plants and roots daily. Record the observations in your science journal.

Flower Parts: Identify the parts of a flower. Record the answers in your science journal.

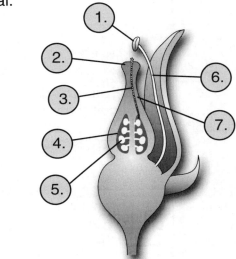

Seeds: Identify the parts of the dicot and monocot seeds. Record the answers in your science journal.

Dicot Seed

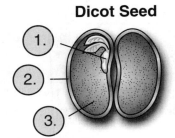

Monocot Seed

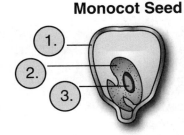

Online Resource: The following animated website will help you learn how to identify trees by studying their leaves, seeds, and fruit. "What tree is that?" Arbor Day Foundation. <http://www.arborday.org/trees/wtit/>

Section 3.3: Animals Word List

amphibian am-**fib**-ē-ən am·phib·i·an	**definition:** a vertebrate that lives part of its life in water and part of its life on land **context:** A salamander is an **amphibian**.
animal **an**-ə-məl an·i·mal	**definition:** a kingdom of multicellular living organisms able to move and respond to stimuli **context:** Mammals are the most complex group of **animals**.
antenna an-**ten**-ə an·ten·na	**definition:** one of a pair of feelers on an arthropod's head used for feeling, tasting, and smelling **context:** Lobsters have two sets of **antennae** (plural for antenna).
bird **bûrd** bird	**definition:** a vertebrate that has both feathers and wings **context:** A **bird** has many adaptations for flight.
cartilage **kär**-tl-ij car·ti·lage	**definition:** a hard flexible tissue **context:** **Cartilage** and bones form the framework of your body.
cocoon kə-**kōōn** co·coon	**definition:** a silk envelope that an insect larva forms about itself and in which it spends the pupa stage **context:** A caterpillar forms a **cocoon** when it becomes a pupa.
cold-blooded kōld-**blud**-id cold–blood·ed	**definition:** an animal having a body temperature the same as the surrounding environment **context:** All reptiles are **cold-blooded**.
egg eg egg	**definition:** the female sex cells **context:** Female moths can lay hundreds of fertilized **eggs** on a single leaf.
exoskeleton ek-sō-**skel**-i-tən ex·o·skel·e·ton	**definition:** an outside skeleton found on arthropods **context:** An **exoskeleton** makes it possible for arthropods to live on land without drying out.
feather **feth**-ər feath·er	**definition:** the light outgrowths covering the body of a bird **context:** When **feathers** wear out, birds shed and grow new ones.
fish **fish** fish	**definition:** a vertebrate that lives its whole life in water **context:** **Fish** live in water and breathe through gills.
gills **gils** gills	**definition:** the organs on fish that get oxygen from the water and remove carbon dioxide from the blood **context:** Fish have **gills** for breathing.
hibernation hī-bər-**nā**-shən hi·ber·na·tion	**definition:** a resting state that helps animals survive the winter **context:** Snakes often group together in underground pits during **hibernation**.
insect **in**-sekt in·sect	**definition:** an animal that has an exoskeleton, three body segments, three pairs of legs, usually two sets of wings, a pair of antennae, and compound eyes **context:** Most known species of animals are **insects**.

Section 3.3: Animals Word List (cont.)

invertebrate in-**vûr**-tə-brāt in·ver·te·brate	**definition:** an animal that does not have a backbone **context:** An earthworm is classified as an **invertebrate** since it does not have a backbone.
kingdom **king**-dəm king·dom	**definition:** a large group of organisms that share certain characteristics **context:** All living things are classified into five **kingdoms**: plants, animals, fungi, protists, and monerans.
larva **lär**-və lar·va	**definition:** a stage in the development of many insects where the caterpillar hatches from an egg **context:** The insect **larva** look like worms.
mammal **mam**-əl mam·mal	**definition:** a vertebrate that gives live birth, feeds its young milk, has hair, and is warm-blooded **context:** The blue whale is the largest **mammal** on Earth.
marsupial mär-**soo**-pē-əl mar·su·pi·al	**definition:** mammal in which the female gives birth to live, undeveloped young that continue to grow inside a pouch **context:** Opossums and kangaroos are **marsupials**.
metamorphosis met-ə-**môr**-fə-sis met·a·mor·pho·sis	**definition:** the change in shape and appearance of an insect or other animal at each stage of its life cycle **context:** Egg, larva, pupa, and adult are the four stages of insect **metamorphosis**.
migration mī-**grā**-shən mi·gra·tion	**definition:** the movement of animals from one place to another during different seasons **context:** The arctic tern's **migration** route covers 22,000 miles.
organism **ôr**-gə-niz-əm or·ga·ni·sm	**definition:** a living thing that carries on the five traits of life: responds, moves, has organized parts, reproduces, grows and develops **context:** Birds, fish, and humans are examples of multicellular **organisms**.
reproduce **rē**-prə-doos re·pro·duce	**definition:** the process of organisms making more of their own kind **context:** All living things **reproduce** to make more of their own species.
reptile **rep**-tīl rep·tile	**definition:** an egg-laying vertebrate with thick, dry skin **context:** A **reptile** is a cold-blooded animal.
skeleton **skel**-i-tən skel·e·ton	**definition:** the framework of bones supporting or protecting an organism **context:** The **skeleton** protects an animal's internal organs.
vertebrate **vûr**-tə-brāt ver·te·brate	**definition:** an animal that has a backbone **context:** A lizard is classified as a **vertebrate** since it has a backbone.
warm-blooded **wôrm**-**blud**-id warm-blood·ed	**definition:** a vertebrate whose body temperature does not change **context:** Birds and mammals are **warm-blooded** because they are able to maintain a constant body temperature.

Section 3.3: Vocabulary Building Activities

Migration: Many animals and insects migrate seasonally or annually. Find out about the unique migration patterns of the animals below. Copy and complete the data table below in your science journal. An example has been provided.

Animal	Description of Migration Pattern
Salmon	Salmon start their lives in freshwater streams, move to the open ocean for their adult lives, and then return to their home stream to lay eggs.
1. Monarch butterfly	
2. Canadian geese	
3. Caribou	
4. Oriole	
5. Manatee	

Online Resources: Some animals travel thousands of miles to reach better conditions of temperature, food, and shelter. The following website provides information concerning several groups of animals that migrate.
"On the Road Again." University of Richmond. <http://oncampus.richmond.edu/academics/ education/projects/webunits/adaptations/migration.html>

Animal Diorama: Choose an animal and use reference materials to learn about the animal's habitat. Use the information to create a diorama. Choose a container such as a small cardboard box or shoe box. Build your diorama working from the back to the front. Decide on a background: sky, plants, and ground. You can paint, draw, or use construction paper. Make 3-D plants and animals from construction paper cut-outs or use small plastic models. Then place large objects such as trees in the box. The smallest objects should be placed closest to the front. Use glue or putty to secure the objects.

Hibernation: Hibernation is the way that animals adapt to the climate and land around them. Animals must be able to live through extreme cold, so some remain dormant (inactive) during the winter months. Below are some of the animals that hibernate during the winter. Copy and complete the data table below in your science journal. Check the correct column for each animal.

Animal	Warm-blooded	Cold-blooded
bears		
hamsters		
frogs		
mice		
turtles		
lizards		
chipmunks		
snakes		
groundhogs		
raccoons		
toads		

Section 3.3: Vocabulary Building Activities (cont.)

Vertebrates: Copy and complete the data table below in your science journal. Provide four examples of each.

Vertebrate	Characteristics	Examples
fish		
amphibians		
reptiles		
birds		
mammals		

Online Resources: Review the animal kingdom at the following interactive website. "Animals Games." Circle 1 Network. <http://www.kidscom.com/games/animal/animal.html>

Tracking Mammals: Wherever mammals live, they produce evidence of their presence. This evidence is most commonly seen in the form of footprints or tracks found in soft, damp soil, mud, sand, or snow. Research an animal to discover the type of tracks it makes. Draw the outline of the animal track on paper. Cut out the pattern. Trace it onto art foam. Cut out the pattern, glue the shapes to a styrofoam-block, and allow the stamp to dry overnight. Practice using the stamp. Press the track on a stamp pad and then on a piece of paper. With a partner, create an animal track story on butcher paper. Stamp the animal tracks to show one animal following another, place tracks farther apart to show an animal running, or cluster the tracks in a small area to show that the animals have found something to eat.

Hangman: Use the animal vocabulary words to play HANGMAN with a partner. Write the letters of the alphabet at the bottom of your paper. Think of a word, and then write the number of dashes that equal the number of letters in the word on your paper. For example, if the word you chose is **hibernation**, write _ _ _ _ _ _ _ _ _ _ _. Your partner then tries to guess the word by naming letters. If the letter guessed is correct, fill in the corresponding dash with the letter. If the guess is incorrect, add a body part to the hangman, starting with a head. The "guesser" gets six tries (head, body, 2 arms, and 2 legs). As your partner guesses letters, cross them off the alphabet, so the letter won't be used again. If your partner guesses the word before the hangman is completed, they win. Start the next round.

WORD: _ _ _ _ _ _ _ _ _ _ _

A B C D E F G H I J K L M
N O P Q R S T U V W X Y Z

Vertebrate vs. Invertebrates: Animals are divided into two groups: vertebrates and invertebrates. Copy and complete the data table below in your science journal. Provide four examples of vertebrates and invertebrates.

Animals	Characteristics	Examples
invertebrate		
vertebrate		

Section 3.4: Life Cycles Word List

adult ə-**dult** a·dult	**definition:** the final stage of an animal's life cycle **context:** Humans have three life cycle stages; birth, youth, and **adult**.
amphibian am-**fib**-ē-ən am·phib·i·an	**definition:** a vertebrate that lives part of its life in water and part of its life on land **context:** A salamander is an **amphibian** that must keep its skin moist.
caterpillar **kat**-ər-pil-ər cat·er·pil·lar	**definition:** the worm-like larva of various insects **context:** The **caterpillar** is the worm-like larva stage of moths and butterflies.
chrysalis **kris**-ə-lis chrys·a·lis	**definition:** the pupa stage of a butterfly's life cycle **context:** The butterfly slowly emerged from the **chrysalis**.
cocoon kə-**kōōn** co·coon	**definition:** a silk envelope that an insect larva forms about itself and in which it passes the pupa stage **context:** The **cocoon** is the pupa stage of a moth's life cycle.
egg eg egg	**definition:** the first stage in an insect's life cycle **context:** Female moths can lay hundreds of fertilized eggs on a single leaf.
embryo **em**-brē-ō em·bry·o	**definition:** an early stage of development in an organism **context:** In humans, a fertilized egg cell can divide into many different cells to form an **embryo**.
exoskeleton ek-sō-**skel**-i-tən ex·o·skel·e·ton	**definition:** an outside skeleton found on arthropods **context:** A grasshopper may shed its **exoskeleton** and form a new one as it grows larger.
fertilization fûr-tl-ī-**zā**-shən fer·til·i·za·tion	**definition:** a sperm cell joining with an egg cell **context:** After **fertilization**, angiosperms produce seeds within the fruit.
flower **flou**-ər flow·er	**definition:** the plant part that performs the job of reproduction **context:** The **flower** is the reproductive structure found in flowering plants.
frog frog frog	**definition:** an amphibian with three life cycle stages: egg, larva (or tadpole) and adult. **context:** A **frog** is an amphibian that begins its life in water as a tadpole.
fruit frōōt fruit	**definition:** the part of plants that carries and protects the seeds **context:** Angiosperms are flowering plants that produce their seeds in a **fruit**.
germination jûr-mə-**nā**-shən ger·mi·na·tion	**definition:** the time it takes for a seed to sprout **context:** Seed **germination** depends on three factors: temperature, moisture, and air.

Section 3.4: Life Cycles Word List (cont.)

gestation je-**stā**-shən ge·sta·tion	**definition:** the process of mammals carrying their young in the womb where the fetus develops until it is born **context:** The period of **gestation** for an elephant is about 645 days.
larva **lär**-və lar·va	**definition:** a stage in the development of many insects where the caterpillar hatches from the egg **context:** The young **larva** feed on leaves.
life cycle **līf** sī-kəl life cy·cle	**definition:** the stages in an organism's life that include birth, development, reproduction, and death **context:** The stages in the **life cycle** of a butterfly include egg, larva, pupa, and adult.
mammal **mam**-əl mam·mal	**definition:** an animal with a life cycle that includes three stages: before birth (gestation), youth, and adult **context:** The blue whale is a **mammal** that goes through three life cycle stages.
metamorphosis met-ə-**môr**-fə-sis met·a·mor·pho·sis	**definition:** the change in shape and appearance of an insect or other animal at each stage of its life cycle **context:** Egg, larva, pupa, and adult are the four stages of **metamorphosis**.
nymph **nimf** nymph	**definition:** a larva of an insect with incomplete metamorphosis **context:** The second stage of development between egg and adult for a dragonfly is the **nymph** stage.
plant **plant** plant	**definition:** an organism with a life cycle that includes seed germination, growing to maturity, flowering, pollination and development of seeds, and seeds falling to the ground **context:** Like animals, **plants** also have life cycles.
pollination **pol**-ə-nā-shən pol·li·na·tion	**definition:** the transfer of a pollen grain to the egg-producing part of a plant **context:** Some flowering plants depend on the wind for **pollination**.
pupa **pyōō**-pə pu·pa	**definition:** the third stage in the life cycle of an insect when it changes from a larva to an adult **context:** The **pupa** stage is part of the life cycle of a butterfly.
reproduce rē-prə-**dōōs** re·pro·duce	**definition:** organisms making more of their own kind **context:** All living things **reproduce**, which creates offspring that look like the parent organisms.
seed **sēd** seed	**definition:** an undeveloped plant with stored food sealed in a protective covering **context:** A **seed** has three parts: seed coat, cotyledon, and embryo.
spore **spôr** spore	**definition:** a reproductive cell of a nonflowering plant **context:** A **spore** from a fern can grow into a new plant.
tadpole **tad**-pōl tad·pole	**definition:** the larva stage of a frog or toad **context:** Frogs begin their lives in water as **tadpoles**.

Section 3.4: Vocabulary Building Activities

Metamorphosis: Cut and glue the pictures below in the correct order to show how a butterfly changes during metamorphosis. Under each box, write the name of the life cycle stage the picture represents. Cut out the completed strip and glue it in your science journal.

stage _____	stage _____	stage _____	stage _____

Frog Life Cycle: Copy and complete the life cycle diagram for a frog in your science journal. Draw a picture in each box and label the life cycle stage it represents.

Life Cycle of a Frog

1.

2.

3.

Online Resources: Review the life cycle of frogs and butterflies at the following animated and interactive website. "Growth and Life Cycles." North Ayrshire Council. <http://www.ers.north-ayrshire.gov.uk/primary/lifecycles.htm>

Word Shape Puzzles: Decide which words from the vocabulary list fit in the word shape blanks. Record the answers in your science journal.

Example: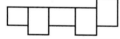

Answer: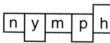

1.

2.

3.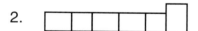

4.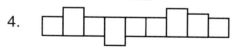

5.

Try: Create five word shape puzzles of your own using the life cycle vocabulary word list. Trade with a partner and solve.

Section 3.4: Vocabulary Building Activities (cont.)

Plant: Draw and describe the five stages in the life cycle of a flowering plant.

Life Cycle Stage

	Description: _____ _____ _____
	Description: _____ _____ _____
	Description: _____ _____ _____
	Description: _____ _____ _____
	Description: _____ _____ _____

Spores: Ferns reproduce from spores, not flowers. On the underside of a fertile fern frond are clusters of brown dots. The dots are made up of many spore cases. Examine a fern frond with spore cases. Use a toothpick to open a spore case. Examine the spores with a magnifying glass. Record observations in your science journal.

Pine Cones: Pine tree seeds are found inside of the cones on the upper surface of each scale. Collect several pine cones. Open pine cones have already dropped their seeds,  so look for and collect cones that are still closed. Look on the ground around pine trees for ripe cones, sometime in the summer or early fall. After you collect the ripe cones, lay them out in the sun to dry. Once dry, the cones will open. Then place them in a paper bag and shake the cones to release the seeds. Examine the seeds and record observations in your science journal.

Section 3.5: Ecology Word List

biome **bī**-ōm bi·ome	**definition:** a large ecosystem, with its own kind of climate, soil, plants, and animals **context:** The tundra is a cold, dry, mostly treeless **biome**.
camouflage **kam**-ə-fläzh cam·ou·flage	**definition:** an adaptation in which an animal protects itself against predators by blending in with the environment **context:** **Camouflage** helps some caterpillars look like twigs.
carnivore **kär**-nə-vôr car·ni·vore	**definition:** an animal that eats other animals **context:** A lion is a **carnivore** that eats the meat of other animals.
coniferous forest kō-**nif**-ər-əs **fôr**-ist co·nif·er·ous for·est	**definition:** a forest of trees that remain green throughout the year, have needle-like leaves, and produce seeds in cones **context:** Pine and fir trees are found in a **coniferous forest** biome.
consumer kən-**soo**-mər con·sum·er	**definition:** an organism that gets energy from eating plants and other animals **context:** All animals are **consumers** because they cannot produce their own food.
deciduous forest di-**sij**-oo-əs **fôr**-ist de·cid·u·ous for·est	**definition:** a forest biome with many kinds of trees that lose their leaves each autumn **context:** Walnut and elm trees may be found in a **deciduous forest**.
decomposer dē-kəm-**pōz**-ər de·com·pos·er	**definition:** an organism that gets energy from dead or decaying organisms **context:** A worm is a **decomposer** that breaks down decaying organisms.
desert **dez**-ərt des·ert	**definition:** a sandy or rocky biome, with little precipitation and little plant life **context:** Animals of the **desert** must be able to survive in a dry climate.
ecology i-**kol**-ə-jē e·col·o·gy	**definition:** the study of how living and nonliving things interact **context:** The students studied the **ecology** of the river system.
ecosystem **ē**-kō-sis-təm e·co·sys·tem	**definition:** the interaction of all the living and nonliving things in an environment **context:** The forest **ecosystem** was damaged by the fire.
endangered species in-**dān**-jərd **spē**-shēz en·dan·gered spe·cies	**definition:** a species that is in danger of becoming extinct **context:** The giant panda is an **endangered species**.
extinct ik-**stingkt** ex·tinct	**definition:** a species that has died out completely **context:** All dinosaurs have died out and become **extinct**.

Section 3.5: Ecology Word List (cont.)

food chain fo͞od chān food chain	**definition:** the path of energy in food from one organism to another **context:** The **food chain** shows how energy moves in one direction from one organism to the next.
food web fo͞od web food web	**definition:** the overlapping food chains in an ecosystem **context:** The **food web** diagram shows the many energy pathways that exist among organisms.
grassland gras-land grass·land	**definition:** a biome where grasses are the main plant life **context:** **Grassland** biomes are home to grazing animals such as the pronghorn antelope and bison.
habitat hab-i-tat hab·i·tat	**definition:** the place where a plant or animal naturally lives and grows **context:** The dolphin lives in a marine **habitat**.
herbivore hûr-bə-vôr her·bi·vore	**definition:** an animal that eats plants and other producers **context:** A cow is classified as an **herbivore** because it eats only plants.
niche nich niche	**definition:** the role of an organism in a community **context:** The **niche** of the honeybee in the ecosystem is to carry pollen from one flower to the next.
omnivore om-nə-vôr om·ni·vore	**definition:** an animal that eats both plants and animals **context:** Humans are omnivores because they eat both plants and animals.
predator pred-ə-tər pred·a·tor	**definition:** an animal that hunts other animals for food **context:** The field mouse was hunted by its **predator**, the hawk.
prey prā prey	**definition:** a living thing that is hunted for food **context:** The lion hunted its **prey**, the zebra.
producer prə-do͞o-sər pro·duc·er	**definition:** an organism that can make its own food **context:** Plants and algae that make their own food are **producers**.
scavenger skav-ən-jər scav·en·ger	**definition:** an animal that feeds on the remains of dead animals **context:** A turkey vulture is a **scavenger** that eats animals that are already dead.
taiga tī-gə tai·ga	**definition:** a cool forest biome of conifers in the upper Northern Hemisphere **context:** The **taiga** biome stretches across a large portion of Canada, Europe, and Asia.
tropical rain forest trop-i-kəl rān fôr-ist trop·i·cal rain for·est	**definition:** a hot biome near the equator, with much rainfall and a wide variety of life **context:** **Tropical rain forests** are located near the equator.
tundra tun-drə tun·dra	**definition:** the treeless plain in the arctic regions, where the ground is frozen all year **context:** The ground of the **tundra** is frozen all year long.

Section 3.5: Vocabulary Building Activities

Biomes: Scientists have divided the world into biomes. Each has its own unique climate, plants, and animals. Copy and complete the table below in your science journal. The first biome has been completed for you.

Biome	Description	Examples of Plants	Examples of Animals
Tundra/ High Mountain	cold, dry, frozen most of the year	mosses and lichens, yellow arctic poppy	caribou, yak, lemming, arctic hare, snowy owl
Forests	coniferous forests: deciduous forests: rain forests:		
Grasslands	steppes: prairies: savannas:		
Deserts	hot and dry		
Aquatic	freshwater: salt water:		

Predator and Prey: Organisms in an ecosystem have special feeding relationships. Copy and complete the predator/prey table in your science journal.

Predator	Prey
lion	wildebeest
1.	
2.	
3.	
4.	
5.	

Relationships: Choose five organisms. Copy and complete the table below in your science journal.

Organism	Habitat	Niche
honeybee	field of clover	carrying pollen
1.		
2.		
3.		
4.		
5.		

Flow of Energy: Food webs represent the flow of energy from one organism to another organism. Examine the food web at right. What would happen if the cat was removed from the food web? Draw a food web in your science journal.

Section 3.5: Vocabulary Building Activities (cont.)

Ecosystem: One of the most obvious places for an ecosystem to be balanced is in its food chain (a diagram of who eats what). All animals have a special place on the food chain. The food chain consists of three levels: producers, consumers, and decomposers. Copy and complete the data table below in your science journal.

Name	Characteristics	Examples
Producers		
Consumers		
Decomposers		

Diet: Each animal has a diet that meets its individual needs. The diets of animals are divided into three groups. Copy and complete the tables below in your science journal.

List two carnivores and the animals they eat.

Carnivores	Animals they eat
1.	
2.	

List two herbivores and the plants they eat.

Herbivores	Plants they eat
1.	
2.	

List two omnivores and the plants and animals they eat.

Omnivores	Plants and animals they eat
1.	
2.	

Food Chain: From a sheet of plain paper, cut out five strips about one inch wide by 8.5 inches long. On each strip, write a different label from the list below. Color that strip the color indicated. Make the strips into circle links and glue the ends together to form a paper food chain. Place the links in the order in which the energy would travel.

OAK TREE (green)   ACORNS FROM OAK TREE (brown)

SQUIRREL (gray)   SUNSHINE (yellow)   FOX (red)

Online Resources: Explore the Amazon through the games and activities at the following website. "Amazon Interactive." Educational Web Adventures. <http://www.eduweb.com/amazon.html>

Section 4.1: Weather Word List

blizzard **bliz**-ərd bliz·zard	**definition:** a severe snowstorm that has strong cold wind filled with fine snow **context:** Visibility is greatly reduced during a **blizzard**.
cirrus **sîr**-əs cir·rus	**definition:** the high, thin, feathery clouds containing ice crystals **context:** Fair weather or incoming storms are associated with **cirrus** clouds.
climate **klī**-mit cli·mate	**definition:** the average weather pattern of a region **context:** Polar, temperate, and tropical are Earth's three **climate** zones.
cloud **kloud** cloud	**definition:** a visible mass of water or ice droplets suspended at a considerable height in the air **context:** A **cloud** is described by its shape.
condensation kon-den-**sā**-shən con·den·sa·tion	**definition:** the changing of a gas into liquid **context:** Fog is the result of **condensation**.
cumulonimbus kyo͞om-yə-lō-**nim**-bəs cu·mu·lo·nim·bus	**definition:** the dark, towering clouds that can produce powerful thunderstorms **context:** Hailstones form at the top of **cumulonimbus** clouds.
cumulus **kyo͞om**-yə-ləs cu·mu·lus	**definition:** the dense, fluffy, white clouds having a flat base **context:** **Cumulus** clouds form in mountain-like shapes when air currents rise.
droplet **drop**-lit drop·let	**definition:** a tiny drop of water **context:** Millions of tiny water **droplets** form a cloud.
evaporation i-vap-ə-**rā**-shən e·vap·o·ra·tion	**definition:** the slow changing of a liquid into a gas **context:** **Evaporation** requires heat energy.
flood **flud** flood	**definition:** a high volume of fast-moving water caused by an enormous amount of rainfall in a short time **context:** The Huang Ho River in China has killed more people than any other river with its **floods**.
fog **fôg** fog	**definition:** a cloud that forms at the surface of the earth **context:** Stratus clouds at ground level are called **fog**.
forecast **fôr**-kast fore·cast	**definition:** a prediction about future weather based on meteorological observations **context:** Satellites help meteorologists **forecast** weather.
hail **hāl** hail	**definition:** ice pellets tossed in high clouds that build up several successive layers and then get heavy and fall to the ground **context:** **Hail** pellets vary from the size of rice grains to melons or softballs.

Section 4.1: Weather Word List (cont.)

hurricane hûr-i-kān hur·ri·cane	**definition:** a tropical cyclone with wind speeds of at least 74 mph or more **context: Hurricanes** are powerful rotating storms formed over tropical oceans.
meteorology mē-tē-ə-**rol**-ə-jē me·te·o·rol·o·gy	**definition:** the study of weather **context: Meteorology** deals with understanding the forces and causes of weather.
precipitation pri-sip-ə-**tā**-shən pre·cip·i·ta·tion	**definition:** the forms of water particles that fall from the atmosphere and reach the ground **context:** Rain and snow are forms of **precipitation**.
rain **rān** rain	**definition:** water falling in drops condensed from vapor in the atmosphere **context: Rain** is liquid water that falls from clouds.
sleet slēt sleet	**definition:** a form of precipitation that falls as frozen or partly frozen rain **context: Sleet** is produced when snow goes through a layer of warm air, melts, and refreezes near the ground.
smog smog smog	**definition:** a type of air pollution produced when smoke and fog mix **context:** Car exhaust fumes contribute to the **smog** problem in Los Angeles, California.
snow snō snow	**definition:** small, white, frozen water crystals formed from the water vapor of the air **context: Snow** falls when the air is cold enough to freeze water vapor.
stratus **strāt**-əs strat·us	**definition:** a type of cloud with smooth layers **context: Stratus** clouds at ground level are called fog.
thunderstorm **thun**-dər-stôrm thun·der·storm	**definition:** a weather condition where lightning and thunder are present **context:** A **thunderstorm** forms inside a warm, moist air mass and along a front.
tornado tôr-**nā**-dō tor·na·do	**definition:** a violent, whirling wind that moves across the ground in a narrow path **context:** A **tornado** forms in low cumulonimbus clouds.
water cycle **wôt**-ər **sī**-kəl wat·er cy·cle	**definition:** the exchange of water between land, bodies of water, and the atmosphere—also known as the hydrologic cycle **context:** Water is continuously moving between the atmosphere and Earth in the **water cycle**.
water vapor **wôt**-ər **vā**-pər wat·er va·por	**definition:** the gaseous state of water **context: Water vapor** is not visible to the naked eye.
weather we**th**-ər weath·er	**definition:** the conditions of the lower atmosphere from day to day at any given place and time **context:** Because Earth has an atmosphere, it experiences **weather**.

Section 4.1: Vocabulary Building Activities

Water Cycle Terms: Identify each picture as an example of condensation, precipitation, or evaporation. Record the answers in your science journal.

1.    2.   3.   4.

Snowflakes: Construct a snowflake catcher by gluing a piece of black felt to a stiff piece of cardboard. Place the snowflake catcher in the freezer, so when the snowflakes are "caught," they will not melt immediately. Go outdoors to catch and observe snowflakes. Use a hand lens to compare and contrast the snowflakes' size and shape. Use reference materials to identify the types of crystal formations that were observed. Record the answers in your science journal. A complete classification of snowflakes can be found at "Winter's Story: Basic Snowflake Identification Field Data." NASA. <www.nasa.gov/pdf/182187main_BasicSnowflakeFieldData.pdf>

Vocabulary Charades: With four other students, write each of the weather vocabulary words on 3 x 5 index cards. Pace the cards face down in a deck on a table. Choose a player to start the game. The first player draws a card. The player then pantomimes the word or phrase on the card to the player to their left, who will get the first chance to guess. (Players are allowed only one guess for each turn.) If their first guess is incorrect, the next player gets to say one answer, and so on. The first player to guess the word or phrase gets a point. The game continues with each player taking a turn, drawing a card, and pantomiming a word until each card has been used. The player with the most points at the end of the game wins.

Cloud Types: There are many different types of clouds. They can be used to forecast the weather. Copy and complete the data table in your science journal.

Type of Cloud	Description	Forecast
1.		
2.		
3.		
4.		

Section 4.2: Seasons Word List

autumn ô-təm au·tumn	**definition:** the season between summer and winter in the Northern Hemisphere; also known as fall **context: Autumn** is the season also known as the fall.
autumnal equinox ô-**tum**-nəl ē-kwə-noks au·tum·nal e·qui·nox	**definition:** the day the sun is directly overhead at noon at the equator in the Northern Hemisphere's fall season **context:** The **autumnal equinox** is around September 21.
equinox ē-kwə-noks e·qui·nox	**definition:** the time when the sun is directly above Earth's equator, which happens two times a year **context: Equinox** times are around March 21 and September 21.
fall fôl fall	**definition:** the season between summer and winter in the Northern Hemisphere; also known as autumn **context:** Maple leaves turn red and orange in the **fall**.
hemisphere hem-i-sfîr hem·i·sphere	**definition:** the halves of Earth as divided by a meridian or the equator **context:** The Northern and Southern **Hemispheres** are divided by the equator; the Eastern and Western are divided by a meridian.
orbit ôr-bit or·bit	**definition:** the pathway of a celestial body as it revolves around another body **context:** The moon is in **orbit** around the earth.
revolution rev-ə-**loo**-shən rev·o·lu·tion	**definition:** the earth's yearly orbit around the sun **context:** Three hundred sixty-five days equal one Earth **revolution**.
solstice sōl-stis sol·stice	**definition:** the point at which the sun is farthest north or south of the equator **context:** A solstice occurs on June 22 and December 22 each year.
spring spring spring	**definition:** the season between winter and summer in the Northern Hemisphere **context:** Weather warms and plants grow in **spring**.
summer sum-ər sum·mer	**definition:** the warmest season of the year in the Northern Hemisphere **context:** The days are longer in **summer**.
vernal equinox vər-nəl ē-kwə-noks ver·nal e·qui·nox	**definition:** the day the sun is directly overhead at noon at the equator in the Northern Hemisphere's spring season **context:** The **vernal equinox** is around March 21.
winter win-tər win·ter	**definition:** the coldest season of the year in the Northern Hemisphere **context:** December through March is considered **winter** in the Northern Hemisphere.
winter solstice win-tər sōl-stis win·ter sol·stice	**definition:** the shortest day of the year in the Northern Hemisphere, occurring on December 21 or 22 **context:** There are more hours of night during the **winter solstice**.
year yîr year	**definition:** a complete revolution of Earth around the sun **context:** There are four seasons in a **year**.

Section 4.2: Vocabulary Building Activities

Earth's Tilted Axis: The seasons are produced by a combination of the earth's tilted axis and its revolution around the sun. Read the questions below and record the answers in your science journal.

1. The day when Earth's Northern Hemisphere is most tilted toward the sun is called the _____.
2. The day when Earth's Northern Hemisphere is most tilted away from the sun is called the _____.

Online Resource: The following animated website shows the earth revolving around the sun in a yearly cycle that produces the four seasons.

"GeoScience animations: Season." Prentice Hall, Inc. <http://esminfo.prenhall.com/science/geoanimations/animations/01_Earth Sun_E2.html>

Seasons: The earth revolves around the sun in a yearly cycle producing the four seasons—summer, autumn, winter, and spring. Copy and complete the data table in your science journal.

First Day of the Season	Date	Tilt of Earth	Length of Days
1. summer solstice			
2. autumnal equinox			
3. winter solstice			
4. vernal equinox			

Summer and Winter: During the summer months, the Northern Hemisphere is tilted toward the sun. During the winter months, the Northern Hemisphere is tilted away from the sun. Copy the diagram below in your science journal. Add Earth's tilted axis to the winter and summer circles. Draw lines with a yellow marker to show how the sun's rays hit Earth during each season.

Winter   **Summer**

Earth   SUN   Earth

When it is winter in the Northern Hemisphere, what season is it in the Southern Hemisphere? Record the answer in your science journal.

Section 4.3: Rocks and Soil Word List

biochemical rock bī-ō-**kem**-i-kəl **rok** bi·o·chem·i·cal rock	**definition:** a sedimentary rock made up of material (such as shells) produced by living organisms **context:** Chalk is an example of a **biochemical rock**.
boulder **bōl**-dər boul·der	**definition:** a large rock **context:** Rocks can be classified by size: **boulders**, cobbles, and pebbles.
chemical weathering **kem**-i-kəl **we***th*-ər-ing chem·i·cal weath·er·ing	**definition:** the process of breaking down rock through chemical changes **context:** **Chemical weathering** changes the chemical composition of rocks.
clay **klā** clay	**definition:** a soil type composed of small particles having plastic (putty-like) properties **context:** **Clay** is found in subsoil.
crystal **kris**-təl crys·tal	**definition:** a solid composed of atoms arranged in an orderly pattern **context:** Minerals possess one of six basic **crystal** shapes.
deposit di-**poz**-it de·pos·it	**definition:** the sediment that settles out of water **context:** **Deposits** settle out of slow-moving water where rivers meet oceans to form deltas.
erosion i-**rō**-zhən e·ro·sion	**definition:** the wearing away of the earth's surface by wind, water, ice, or gravity **context:** Planting trees and grasses slows **erosion**.
fossil **fos**-əl fos·sil	**definition:** the remains of an ancient, once living organism preserved in rock **context:** **Fossils** of long-dead animals contain clues to the past.
gem **jem** gem	**definition:** a highly prized, valuable mineral **context:** An emerald is a valuable **gem**.
horizon hə-**rī**-zn ho·ri·zon	**definition:** one of the layers of the soil that have different properties **context:** Four **horizons** can be found in mature soil.
humus **hyōō**-məs hu·mus	**definition:** the brown or black part of soil formed from decaying plant or animal matter **context:** **Humus** is found in topsoil.
igneous rock **ig**-nē-əs **rok** ig·ne·ous rock	**definition:** rocks formed when molten lava cools **context:** **Igneous** rocks are one of the three classifications of rocks.
mechanical weathering mi-**kan**-i-kəl **we***th*-ər-ing me·chan·i·cal weath·er·ing	**definition:** the physical forces that break down rock **context:** **Mechanical weathering** can be seen when expanding ice creates enough force to break a rock into smaller pieces.
metamorphic rock met-ə-**môr**-fik **rok** met·a·mor·phic rock	**definition:** rocks formed when sedimentary or igneous rocks undergo a change due to pressure or heat in the earth **context:** **Metamorphic rocks** are found deep in the earth.

Section 4.3: Rocks and Soil Word List (cont.)

mineral min-ər-əl min·er·al	**definition:** a naturally occurring, non-living solid with a specific chemical composition and crystal structure **context:** Quartz is a **mineral**.
Mohs' scale Mōz skāl Mohs' scale	**definition:** a list of minerals of varying hardness **context:** The hardness of the mineral topaz can be measured using the **Mohs' scale**.
ore ôr ore	**definition:** a mineral that contains a valuable substance in it, such as silver or iron **context:** Mineral **ores** provide raw materials to make everything from toothpaste to CD players.
paleontologist pā-lē-on-**tol**-ə-jist pa·le·on·tol·o·gist	**definition:** a person who studies fossils **context:** A **paleontologist** may study fossils to reconstruct Earth's living past.
pebble peb-əl peb·ble	**definition:** a small, smooth, rounded rock **context:** Rocks can be classified by size: boulders, cobbles, and **pebbles**.
rock rok rock	**definition:** a naturally occurring combination of minerals **context:** The earth's crust consists of three types of **rock**—igneous, sedimentary, and metamorphic.
rock cycle rok sī-kəl rock cy·cle	**definition:** a gradual and steady change of rock in the earth's crust to igneous, sedimentary, or metamorphic rock **context:** The **rock cycle** is a never-ending series of processes where rock is changed from one type to another—igneous, sedimentary, and metamorphic.
sand sand sand	**definition:** the rock and mineral particles smaller than two millimeters in diameter **context:** Ocean shorelines are made of **sand**.
sediment sed-ə-**ment** sed·i·ment	**definition:** the pieces of material carried and deposited by water or wind **context:** After the rainstorm, the river carried **sediment** to the lake.
sedimentary rock sed-ə-**men**-tə-rē rok sed·i·men·ta·ry rock	**definition:** rocks formed by the layering of sediments **context:** **Sedimentary rocks** are formed from particles created by the weathering and erosion of existing rocks.
silt silt silt	**definition:** very small soil particles that can be picked up and carried by wind and water **context:** Many of the smaller lakes are now filled with **silt**.
soil ôil soil	**definition:** a mixture of crushed rock and pieces of organic material from plants and animals that covers some areas of the crust **context:** Fertile **soil** helps plants grow.
weathering we*th*-ər-ing weath·er·ing	**definition:** the mechanical or chemical breaking of rock into smaller pieces that eventually decay to soil **context:** **Weathering** changes the earth's surface over time.

Section 4.3: Vocabulary Building Activities

Crystals: Minerals are made of crystals. Crystals form in one of six distinct shapes. Examine the crystal shape of salt. Sprinkle salt on black paper. Examine the crystals with a magnifying glass. Draw a sketch of the salt crystal in your science journal. Compare the shape of the salt crystals to the six basic crystal shapes below. What is the shape of the salt crystals? Record the answer in your science journal.

Cubic

Monoclinic

Tetragonal

Orthorhombic

Triclinic

Hexagonal

Earth's Surface: Weathering and erosion are both actions that change the face of the earth. Copy and complete the data table in your science journal.

Result	Action
1. Grand Canyon	
2. Soil formation	
3. Mississippi Delta	
4. Carlsbad Caverns	
5. Features on the Great Sphinx are disappearing	

Online Resources: Learn more about rocks and soil at the following interactive websites. "Rocks and Soil" and "The Dirt on Soil." Discovery Education. <http://www.bbc.co.uk/schools/scienceclips/ages/7_8/rocks_soils.shtml>

Fossils: Look at the cross section of rock layers below. Record the answer to the following question in your science journal.

Which fossil is oldest: A, B, or C? Explain your answer.

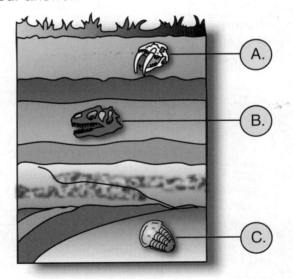

Rocks: There are three main types of rocks—**igneous**, **sedimentary**, and **metamorphic**. Each rock type is formed differently and has identifiable characteristics. There are many examples of each type of rock (sandstone is an example of a sedimentary rock). Create a data table in your science journal that lists the following data for each type of rock.

Type of Rock	How Rock Was Formed	Characteristics of the Rock Type	Where Found	Example of Rock Type

Section 4.4: Changes in the Earth's Surface Word List

acid rain as-id **rān** acid rain	**definition:** the rain caused by air pollutants when they mix with water in the air **context: Acid rain** can poison lakes and rivers.
asthenosphere as-**then**-ə-sfîr as·then·o·sphere	**definition:** the plastic-like zone in the earth's mantle below the lithosphere, or the crust **context:** The **asthenosphere** is denser than the lithosphere.
core kôr core	**definition:** the innermost portion of the earth that consists of solid iron and nickel **context:** Earth has an inner and an outer **core**.
crust **krust** crust	**definition:** the outer layer of Earth that is mostly solid rock; also known as the lithosphere **context:** The earth's **crust** contains over 4,000 known minerals.
deformation dē-fôr-**mā**-shən de·for·ma·tion	**definition:** the stress and strain in the earth that causes the crust to fracture, fault, or fold **context:** The San Andreas fault is the best known example of **deformation** in the United States.
deposition di-**poz**-i-shən de·pos·i·tion	**definition:** the process where sediments are left in new locations **context:** The dust storm left a **deposition** of sand against the wall of the old fort.
earthquake **ûrth**-kwāk earth·quake	**definition:** the shaking, trembling, or rolling movements usually caused by bodies of rock slipping past each other at faults **context:** An **earthquake** can occur at the earth's surface, in the lithosphere, or in the asthenosphere.
epicenter **ep**-i-sen-tər ep·i·cen·ter	**definition:** the spot on the earth's surface that is above the focus of an earthquake **context:** The **epicenter** is on the earth's surface directly above the earthquake's focus.
erosion i-**rō**-zhən e·ro·sion	**definition:** the wearing away of earth's surface by wind, water, ice, or gravity **context:** Planting trees and grasses slows **erosion**.
fault **fôlt** fault	**definition:** a crack in the earth's crust where bodies of rock rub against each other, releasing energy waves during an earthquake **context:** Earthquakes occur along a **fault**.
focus **fō**-kəs fo·cus	**definition:** the exact place in the earth where an earthquake begins **context:** The focus of an earthquake may be deep underground.
lava **lä**-və la·va	**definition:** the molten rock from a volcano **context:** Once exposed at the surface, magma becomes **lava**.
lithosphere **li**-thə-sfîr lith·o·sphere	**definition:** another name for the crust; the outer layer of Earth that is mostly solid rock **context:** The **lithosphere** is the layer at Earth's surface.

Section 4.4: Changes in the Earth's Surface Word List (cont.)

magma **mag**-mə mag·ma	**definition:** the molten rock that makes up Earth's mantle **context: Magma** that flows from volcanoes is called lava.
mantle **man**-tl man·tle	**definition:** the layer of Earth that lies between the crust and the core **context:** The **mantle** is the thickest layer of Earth.
meander mē-**an**-dər me·an·der	**definition:** the bend or s-shaped curve formed by fast moving currents of water in a mature stream **context:** The curving sides of streams are called **meanders**.
mountain **moun**-tən moun·tain	**definition:** a landmass that projects conspicuously above its surroundings **context:** A **mountain** is much larger than a hill.
ocean ō-shən o·cean	**definition:** the bodies of salt water covering 72 percent of earth's surface **context:** Shorelines are constantly changing because of the **ocean's** waves, tides, and currents.
Pangaea pan-**jē**-ə Pan·gae·a	**definition:** the name of the ancient landmass believed to have broken up into today's continents **context:** Scientists think that the continents were once joined together in one supercontinent, **Pangaea**.
Richter scale **rik**-tər **skāl** Rich·ter scale	**definition:** a scale used to describe how much energy is released by an earthquake **context:** In 1923, an earthquake measuring 8.3 on the **Richter scale** occurred in Tokyo, Japan.
Ring of Fire **ring** uv **fīr** ring of fire	**definition:** a ring formed by active volcano and earthquake hotspots that circles the rim of the Pacific Ocean **context:** Active volcanoes may be found in the **Ring of Fire**.
runoff **run**-ôf run·off	**definition:** the water that runs off the surface of the earth into rivers, streams, or lakes **context:** Grass and other plants tend to slow down the amount of **runoff**.
seismograph **sīz**-mə-graf seis·mo·graph	**definition:** an instrument that records earthquake waves **context:** Seismologists use **seismographs** to determine an earthquake's magnitude.
tsunami tsōō-**nä**-mē tsu·na·mi	**definition:** a large ocean wave caused by an underwater earthquake or landslide with waves reaching 30 meters **context:** The United States developed the **Tsunami** Warning System in 1948.
volcano vol-**kā**-nō vol·ca·no	**definition:** a place in the earth's surface where hot magma is forced up, forming a mountain that erupts and builds upward **context:** Hawaii's Kilauea **volcano** is the world's most active volcano.

Section 4.4: Vocabulary Building Activities

Volcanoes: Scientists have divided volcanoes into three main groups—cinder cone, shield, and composite. They are classified based on shape and type of material they are built of. Copy and complete the data table below in your science journal.

Type	Description	Example (Name of the Volcano and Location)
1. cinder cone		
2. shield		
3. composite		

Online Resource: Create your own earthquake at the following interactive website. "Earthquake: Make a Quake." Discovery Communications, LLC. <dsc.discovery.com/guides/planetearth/earthquake/interactive/interactive.html>

CrossWord Puzzle: Choose 12 vocabulary words to use for your puzzle. Select one of the words. On 1-cm grid paper using a pencil, write one letter in each box forming your word horizontally (across) on the paper. Write another word vertically (down) on the grid paper so the words overlap where they have a common letter. Continue adding words to your puzzle until you have used all 12 words. Starting with 1, assign a number to each horizontal word and then the vertical words. At the bottom of the grid paper, write a definition for each of the words. Organize the definitions into "across" and "down" columns using the numbers on the puzzle grid. Trace around the squares you used with a marker. Erase the letters in each square. Trade your puzzle with a partner and solve.

Earth's Layers: The diagram shows Earth's layers (mantle, inner core, outer core, and crust). Identify the layers and their characteristics. Record the answers in your science journal.

Ring of Fire: The Ring of Fire is a chain of over 300 volcanoes around the rim of the Pacific Ocean. Use a map to locate the following volcanoes. Copy and complete the data table in your science journal.

Volcano	Location
1. Mount Tambora	
2. Mount Fuji	
3. Mauna Loa	
4. Mount Katmai	
5. Mount St. Helens	
6. Paricutin	
7. Aconcagua	

Section 5.1: Objects in the Sky Word List

asteroid **as**-tə-roid as·ter·oid	**definition:** a large rock in the solar system; often called a minor planet **context:** An **asteroid** is too small to be a planet.
astronomy ə-**stron**-ə-mē a·stron·o·my	**definition:** the study of the planets, stars, galaxies, and all other objects in space **context:** Exploring **astronomy** and other space-related topics is part of science class.
aurora ə-**rôr**-ə au·ror·a	**definition:** the colorful light seen over the polar regions **context:** The **aurora** borealis, visible in the Northern Hemisphere, is sometimes called the Northern Lights.
celestial sphere sə-**les**-chəl **sfîr** ce·les·tial sphere	**definition:** an imaginary dome surrounding Earth used to help astronomers explain where objects are found in the sky **context:** Astronomers think of the **celestial sphere** as an imaginary bubble surrounding the earth that contains the sun, moon, stars, and planets.
coma **kō**-mə co·ma	**definition:** the cloud of dust and gases surrounding the nucleus of a comet **context:** The **coma** is part of the head of a comet.
comet **kom**-it com·et	**definition:** a combination of ice, dust, and rock material that moves in an orbit around the sun **context:** A **comet** has a head and long, flowing, vapor tail.
constellation kon-stə-**lā**-shən con·stel·la·tion	**definition:** star groups that resemble familiar objects or characters **context:** The Big and Little Dipper are **constellations**.
dwarf star **dwôrf stär** dwarf star	**definition:** a small star **context:** A **dwarf star** is only a little larger than Earth.
impact im-**pakt** im·pact	**definition:** a collision of two objects **context:** The **impact** of a meteorite on the surface of the moon can leave a crater.
light-year **līt yîr** light-year	**definition:** the distance light travels in one year **context:** A star's distance from Earth is measured in **light-years**.
magnitude **mag**-ni-tōōd mag·ni·tude	**definition:** the brightness of a star as seen from Earth **context:** A star's **magnitude** depends on its size, temperature, and distance from Earth.
meteor **mē**-tē-ôr me·te·or	**definition:** a meteoroid (space rock or dust from a comet or broken-up asteroid) that burns up in the earth's atmosphere **context:** Shooting stars are actually **meteors**.
meteorite **mē**-tē-ə-rīt me·te·o·rite	**definition:** a meteoroid that hits the earth's surface **context:** **Meteorites** are believed to be debris from asteroid collisions.

Section 5.1: Objects in the Sky Word List (cont.)

meteoroid mē-tē-ə-roid me·te·or·oid	**definition:** a space rock or dust from a comet or broken-up asteroid **context:** Many **meteoroids** enter Earth's atmosphere each year.
meteor shower mē-tē-ôr shou-ər me·te·or show·er	**definition:** an event where a large number of meteoroids burn up as they enter the earth's atmosphere **context:** The Leonids, a spectacular **meteor shower**, can be seen each November.
nebula **neb**-yə-lə neb·u·la	**definition:** any of the glowing clouds of gas or dust reflecting the light of nearby stars **context:** A **nebula** can be seen in the belt of the Orion constellation.
nova **nō**-və no·va	**definition:** a star that suddenly flares up to many times its original brightness before fading again **context:** The **nova** was a result of the explosion on the surface of a white dwarf star.
Polaris pə-**lar**-is Po·lar·is	**definition:** the North Star, always above Earth's North Pole **context:** **Polaris**, or the North Star, is the last star in the handle of the Little Dipper.
pulsar **pul**-sär pul·sar	**definition:** a star that sends energy out in pulses **context:** A **pulsar** appears to flash on and off many times a second.
quasar **kwā**-zär qua·sar	**definition:** an object about the size of a star that gives off huge amounts of energy **context:** The nearest **quasar** to Earth is billions of light-years away.
satellite **sat**-l-īt sat·el·lite	**definition:** an object in space that revolves around a planet **context:** The moon is Earth's natural **satellite**.
shooting star **shoot**-ing **stär** shoot·ing star	**definition:** a meteoroid (space rock or dust from a comet or broken-up asteroid) that burns up in the earth's atmosphere; a meteor **context:** **Shooting stars** are actually meteors.
sky **skī** sky	**definition:** the part of the atmosphere or of outer space visible from the surface of Earth or any other planet **context:** Astronomers think of the **sky** or outer space as the place where the sun, stars, planets, and the moon travel.
star **stär** star	**definition:** a distant sun glowing from heat produced by nuclear reactions at its center **context:** Planets are closer to Earth than the **stars** are.
Ursa Major **ûr**-sə **mā**-jər Ur·sa Ma·jor	**definition:** a constellation that can be seen all year in the Northern Hemisphere **context:** **Ursa Major** is also known as the Great Bear and is part of the Big Dipper constellation.

Section 5.1: Vocabulary Building Activities

Halley's Comet: The best known comet is Halley's Comet. It appears about every 74 to 79 years. The next predicted appearance of Halley's Comet is the year 2061. Identify the parts of a comet. Record the answers in your science journal.

Constellations: The following are constellations you can see in the night sky. Record the name of each constellation in your science journal.

1. 2. 3. 4. 5. 6.

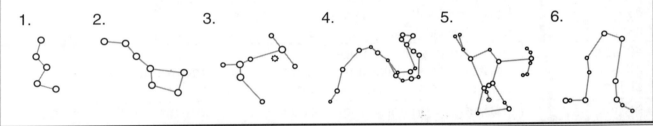

Meteor Shower: "Falling stars" or "shooting stars" are streaks of light you can sometimes see in the night sky. They are caused by tiny bits of dust and rock called meteors falling into the Earth's atmosphere and burning up. The Leonid, one of the most spectacular meteor showers, can be seen nightly between November 13 to November 21 each year.

Viewing Tips

- Viewing is best away from the city lights.
- Watch late in the nighttime.
- Watch on a clear night.
- Look north, just above the tree line.

Stars: Learn how to find the Big Dipper in the summer night sky at the following website.
"Stars." Ducks Unlimited.
<www.greenwing.org/newgreenwing/activities/stars%20copy/stars1.htm>

Venn Diagram: Compare and contrast two types of space rock—meteor and meteorite. Copy and complete the Venn diagram in your science journal.

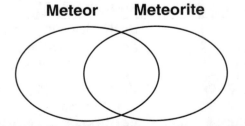

Section 5.2: Earth, Sun, and Moon Word List

axis ak-sis ax·is	**definition:** an imaginary line around which the earth spins **context:** Earth rotates on its **axis** from west to east.
core kôr core	**definition:** the central part of the sun **context:** At the **core** of the sun, hydrogen changes to helium.
corona kə-rō-nə co·ro·na	**definition:** the outermost part of the sun's atmosphere **context:** The white light seen around the sun during a solar eclipse is the **corona**.
crater krā-tər cra·ter	**definition:** a bowl-shaped hole on the moon **context:** Scientists believe the **craters** on the moon were caused by meteorites.
day dā day	**definition:** the complete rotation of Earth on its axis; 24 hours; the daylight hours **context:** One rotation of the earth is a **day** consisting of 24 hours.
Earth ûrth earth	**definition:** the third planet from the sun in the solar system **context: Earth** is traveling around the sun while it is also being orbited by the moon.
ellipse i-**lips** el·lipse	**definition:** an oval shape **context:** The orbits of the planets are not circular but resemble an elongated circle called an **ellipse**.
gravity grav-i-tē grav·i·ty	**definition:** the force that keeps planets in orbit around the sun and governs the rest of the motion in the solar system **context: Gravity** holds us on the earth's surface.
lunar eclipse loo-nər i-**klips** lu·nar e·clipse	**definition:** when the Earth passes between the moon and the sun, casting a shadow on the moon **context: Lunar eclipses** occur only when the moon is full.
mare mä-rā ma·re	**definition:** smooth places on the surface of the moon **context:** The Sea of Serenity on the moon is a flat plain called a **mare**.
moon mōon moon	**definition:** a celestial body that revolves around a planet **context:** Earth's **moon** has a barren, rocky surface.
night nīt night	**definition:** the time from dusk to dawn when no sunlight is visible. **context:** During one rotation of Earth, there is one period of daylight and one **night**.
orbit ôr-bit or·bit	**definition:** the path the moon, planets, asteroids, and comets follow as they travel around the sun **context:** Earth's **orbit** around the sun is an oval shape.
penumbra pi-**num**-brə pe·num·bra	**definition:** the outside fringe of the shadow cast by Earth during a lunar eclipse **context:** The **penumbra** is an area of lighter shadow than the umbra during a lunar eclipse.

Section 5.2: Earth, Sun, and Moon Word List (cont.)

phase fāz phase	**definition:** one of the different shapes the moon appears to be as seen from the earth **context:** A full moon is one **phase** of the moon.
photosphere fō-tə-sfîr pho·to·sphere	**definition:** the surface of the sun **context:** Heat and light move outward from the core to the **photosphere** of the sun.
revolution rev-ə-lōō-shən rev·o·lu·tion	**definition:** the movement of planets around the sun **context:** Every 365 $\frac{1}{4}$ days, the earth completes one **revolution** around the sun.
rotation rō-tā-shən ro·ta·tion	**definition:** the spinning of an object **context:** Earth **rotates** on its axis once every 24 hours.
satellite sat-l-īt sat·el·lite	**definition:** an object in space that revolves around a planet **context:** The moon is Earth's natural **satellite**.
season sē-zən sea·son	**definition:** a major division of the year—spring, summer, autumn, or winter **context:** The **seasons** are produced by a combination of the earth's tilted axis and its revolution around the sun.
shadow shad-ō shad·ow	**definition:** a region of darkness where light is blocked **context:** During a lunar eclipse, the earth casts a **shadow** on the moon.
solar eclipse sō-lər i-klips so·lar e·clipse	**definition:** when the moon passes between the sun and Earth **context:** The shadow of the moon is cast on the earth during a **solar eclipse**.
solar flare sō-lər flâr so·lar flare	**definition:** the bright areas in the sun's atmosphere from which hot gases shoot out into space **context:** **Solar flares** seem to interfere with radio signals.
sun sən sun	**definition:** a star that is the source of light and heat for the planets in a solar system; our sun is called Sol **context:** The **sun** is a star made of gases so hot they glow, giving off light.
sunspot sən-spot sun·spot	**definition:** a dark spot on the sun **context:** A **sunspot** is a place on the sun where the gases have cooled and do not give off as much light as other areas.
tide tīd tide	**definition:** the rise and fall of ocean water, caused by the moon **context:** **Tides** occur along every ocean coast.
umbra **um**-brə um·bra	**definition:** the darker, center part of the shadow cast by the earth during a lunar eclipse **context:** The **umbra** is caused by the earth during a lunar eclipse.
year yîr year	**definition:** a complete revolution of Earth around the sun **context:** One **year** on Earth is 365 $\frac{1}{4}$ days long.

Section 5.2: Vocabulary Building Activities

Phases of the Moon: The diagram below shows four phases of the moon as seen from Earth. Identify each phase and record the answers in your science journal.

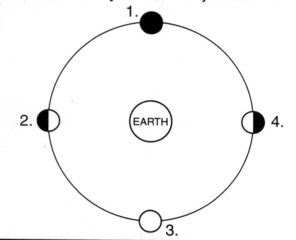

Eclipse: As the earth revolves around the sun and the moon around the earth, they occasionally align so the sunlight is blocked. Examine the diagrams below. Identify the type of eclipse shown. Record the answers in your science journal.

1.
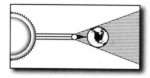

2.
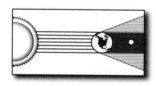

Sun: Identify the parts of the sun. Record the answers in your science journal.

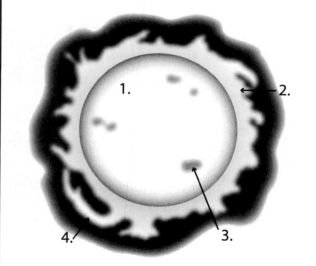

Online Resource: Learn more about a solar eclipse at the following animated website.
"Moon Shadow: Solar Eclipse." Scholastic Inc. <http://teacher.scholastic.com/ activities/science/moon_interactives. htm>

Craters: The moon's surface is dotted with small craters. When meteoroids hit the surface of the moon, a large amount of energy is produced. The energy is absorbed by the ground. This energy causes the soil to move and creates different sized and shaped impact craters.

Activity: Create impact craters similar to the ones on the surface of the moon. Drop different size rocks in a box of sand from varying heights. Copy and complete the data table in your science journal.

Rock Size (cm)	Height From Sand	Describe the Crater
1.		
2.		
3.		
4.		
5.		

Section 5.3: Solar System Word List

asteroid belt as-tə-roid **belt** as·te·roid belt	**definition:** the concentration of asteroids between Mars and Jupiter **context:** The **asteroid belt** separates the inner planets from the outer planets in our solar system.
astronaut as-trə-nôt as·tro·naut	**definition:** a person who travels in space **context:** Sally Ride was the first woman U.S. **astronaut**.
astronomy ə-**stron**-ə-mē a·s·tron·o·my	**definition:** the study of the planets, stars, galaxies, and all other objects in space. **context:** Scientists study **astronomy** to find out about all the objects in space.
black hole blak hōl black hole	**definition:** an area in space from which light cannot escape **context:** A **black hole** is an area in space where star material seems to disappear.
cosmos koz-mōs cos·mos	**definition:** another name for space or the universe **context:** Images from the Hubble Space Telescope help scientists map the **cosmos**.
Earth ûrth Earth	**definition:** the third planet from the sun in our solar system **context:** **Earth** has one moon.
extrasolar planet ek-strə-sō-lər **plan**-it ex·tra·so·lar plan·et	**definition:** planets outside our solar system **context:** Most of the **extrasolar** planets are Jupiter-sized or larger.
galaxy gal-ək-sē gal·ax·y	**definition:** a group of billions of stars **context:** **Galaxies** have different shapes.
Jupiter joo-pi-tər Ju·pi·ter	**definition:** the fifth planet from the sun in our solar system **context:** **Jupiter** is the largest planet in our solar system.
Mars März Mars	**definition:** the fourth planet from the sun in our solar system **context:** **Mars** is similar to Earth and, therefore, has seasons.
Mercury mər-kyə-rē Mer·cu·ry	**definition:** the first planet from the sun in our solar system **context:** It takes **Mercury** 59 Earth days to rotate once.
Milky Way Galaxy mil-kē wā gal-ək-sē Mil·ky Way Gal·ax·y	**definition:** the galaxy in which Earth and our solar system is located **context:** Our solar system is located in the **Milky Way Galaxy**.
moon moon moon	**definition:** a celestial body that revolves around a planet **context:** Mars has two **moons** orbiting it.
NASA na-sa Na·sa	**definition:** the abbreviation for National Aeronautics and Space Administration **context:** Official U.S. space projects are handled by **NASA**.

Section 5.3: Solar System Word List (cont.)

Neptune nep-tōōn Nep·tune	**definition:** the eighth planet from the sun in our solar system **context: Neptune** rotates on a nearly upright axis.
planet **plan**-it plan·et	**definition:** an object bigger than an asteroid orbiting a star **context: Planets** travel in elliptical orbits around the sun.
planetarium pla-nə-**ter**-ē-əm plan·e·tar·i·um	**definition:** a theater built for presenting shows about astronomy and the night sky **context:** Scenes of stars, planets, and other celestial objects are projected on the dome-shaped screen of a **planetarium** to simulate the motions of space.
ring **ring** ring	**definition:** a band of dust and other small particles orbiting around a planet **context:** Saturn, Jupiter, Uranus, and Neptune have **rings**.
Saturn **Sat**-ərn Sat·urn	**definition:** the sixth planet from the sun in our solar system **context:** Scientists believe **Saturn** has at least 60 moons.
solar system sō-lər **sis**-təm so·lar sys·tem	**definition:** the sun and all the objects revolving around the sun **context:** There are eight planets and many other objects in our **solar system**.
space spās space	**definition:** the area outside Earth's atmosphere **context:** The first U.S. astronaut to travel in **space** was Alan Shepard.
spacecraft spās-kraft space·craft	**definition:** a vehicle able to travel in outer space **context:** The Cassini **spacecraft** left Earth in 1997 and arrived at Saturn in 2004.
sun sən sun	**definition:** a star that is the source of light and heat for the planets in a solar system; our sun is called Sol **context:** The **sun** is a star made of gases so hot they glow, giving off light.
telescope **tel**-ə-skōp tel·e·scope	**definition:** an instrument used for viewing faraway objects, such as planets and stars **context: Telescopes** help scientists see distant planets and stars.
universe yōo-nə-vûrs u·ni·verse	**definition:** the planets, stars, and everything that exist in space **context:** The **universe** is endless.
Uranus yûr-ə-nəs Ur·a·nus	**definition:** the seventh planet from the sun in our solar system **context: Uranus** is the third largest planet in our solar system.
Venus vē-nəs Ve·nus	**definition:** the second planet from the sun in our solar system **context:** The atmosphere on **Venus** is made of clouds containing tiny droplets of acid.

Section 5.3: Vocabulary Building Activities

Solar System: There are eight planets in our solar system. Examine the diagram at right. Identify each planet. Record the answers in your science journal.

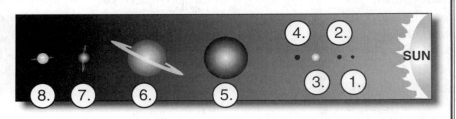

Online Resource: Learn more about the solar system at the following interactive website. "Solar System." Kids Know It Network. <http://www.kidsastronomy.com/solar_system.htm>

The Planets: Create a mnemonic device to help you remember the planets in their correct order from the sun.

Planet	Example	My Mnemonic
Mercury	My	M
Venus	Very	V
Earth	Educated	E
Mars	Mother	M
Jupiter	Just	J
Saturn	Served	S
Uranus	Us	U
Neptune	Nachos	N

Space Exploration: Research space exploration. Draw a time line in your science journal. Place the following events and the year they occurred in the correct order on your time line.

- John Glenn, first American to orbit Earth
- Edward White, the first U.S. space walk
- Sally Ride, the first U.S. woman to travel in space
- Neil Armstrong and Edwin "Buzz" Aldrin, the first landing on the moon, and the first moon walk
- Pioneer 10 is launched, designed to familiarize alien life with humans
- Alan Shepard, the first U.S. astronaut in space

Planet Facts: Each planet is unique. Copy and complete the data table in your science journal.

Planet	Symbol	Distance from Sun	Length of Day	Length of Year	Number of Moons	Rings?
Mercury						yes/no
Venus						yes/no
Earth						yes/no
Mars						yes/no
Jupiter						yes/no
Saturn						yes/no
Uranus						yes/no
Neptune						yes/no

Index

Index (cont.)

Index (cont.)

More Science Words

action force	cell division	cross-pollination
adapt	cell metabolism	current
adaptation	cellular respiration	cytokinesis
air mass	centromere	daughter cell
air pressure	ceramic-fiber square	decibel
algae	characteristic	dependent variable
alkaline	charge	desalination
allele	chemical	dew point
alternating current	chemical bond	dichotomous key
ametabolous	chemical energy	diffraction
amino acid	chemical equation	direct current
amoeba	chemical formula	dissolve
amplitude	chemical reaction	diversity
analyze	chemical spoon	dominant
angiosperm	chromatid	dry cell
aquifer	chromatography	echo sounder
Aqua-Lung	chromosphere	ecological succession
arthropod	cilia	electrical charge
asexual reproduction	classification hierarchy	electric current
atmosphere	classify	electric field
atmospheric pressure	climax community	electric motor
atomic mass	clone	electromagnetic wave
atomic number	colloid	electromagnetic spectrum
attract	color	electron cloud
autotrophy	combustion	electron dot diagram
bacteria	commensalism	El Niño
barometric pressure	community	energy level
battery	compare	energy pyramid
beaker	competition	endoskeleton
behavior	complete metamorphosis	endothermic reaction
bias	compressed wave	environment
biodiversity	concave	enzyme
biosphere	conduction	Erlenmeyer flask
biotic factor	conjunction	estimate
blade	conserving energy	euglena
boiling point	constant	evaporating dish
bond	continental shelf	exosphere
budding	continental slope	exothermic reaction
Bunsen burner	controlled variable	extrusive
cast	convection	fern
catalyst	convection current	fibrous root
cave	convex	fissure
celestial	coral reef	flagella

flight	hydroelectric energy	mid-ocean ridge
float	hydrologic cycle	mirror
Florence flask	incomplete metamorphosis	mitosis
fluid	independent variable	model
focal point	infrared wave	mold
fold	infer	monera
formulate	inherited trait	mortar and pestle
fossil fuel	inner core	motor
fracture	interference	mutation
freeze	intrusive	mutualism
frequency	ion	nebulae
frond	ionosphere	net-veined leaf
front	iron ring	neutron star
fuel cell	isomer	noble gas
fulcrum	isotope	nonmetal
function	jet stream	nonrenewable resource
fungi	Kelvin	nonvascular
fungus	kinetic energy	nuclear energy
funnel	latent heat	nucleolus
gamete	law	ocean floor
gametophyte	lens	ohms
gamma ray	litmus paper	opaque
gene	loudness	orbital plane
generator	luminous intensity	outer core
genetics	magnetic domain	ovary
genome	magnetism	oxidation
genotype	magnetite	ozonosphere
geology	magnetosphere	parallel circuit
geothermal energy	marine	parallel vein
global warming	mass number	paramecium
greenhouse effect	measurement	parasitism
groundwater	mechanical wave	pathogen
guard cell	medium	petiole
gymnosperm	meiosis	petroleum
herbaceous	melting point	phenotype
heredity	Mendel, Gregor	photovoltaic
hertz	Mendelian trait	pioneer community
heterogeneous mixture	mesosphere	pioneer species
heterotrophy	metal	pipet
homogeneous mixture	metalloid	pitch
host	microbe	plankton
humidity	microscopic	plasma
hybrid	microwave	plasma membrane

More Science Words (cont.)

pollution
population
potential energy
power
precision
prevailing winds
prism
product
protist
protozoa
Punnett square
qualitative
quantitative
radiant energy
radiation
radioactive
radio wave
rainbow
rate of reaction
reactant
reaction force
recessive
recycle
relative humidity
renewable resource
repel
resistance
respiration
results
rhizoid
rhizome
ring stand
saline
sand dune
saturated
seed coat
self-pollination
series circuit
sex cell
sexual reproduction
shoreline
simple leaf
sink

solar energy
solubility
solution
solvent
sonar
spatula
species
stalactite
stalagmite
stimulus
stratosphere
submarine canyon
supernova
suspension
switch
symbiosis
symmetry
system
taproot
taxonomy
tectonic plates
terrestrial planet
theory
thermosphere
tidal energy
toxin
trade winds
traits
transformer
translucent
transpiration
transverse wave
tree
trench
triple beam balance
tropism
troposphere
turbine
ultraviolet light
vacuum
vapor
variable
vascular

velocity
Venn diagram
vibration
virus
visible light
voltage
water
watt
wavelength
westerlies
wilderness
wildlife
wind
wire
woody
X-ray

Answer Keys

Chapter 1—Scientific Inquiry Vocabulary
Section 1.1: Scientific Method (page 7)
Science Fair Project Topic:
Topics number 2 and 3 are too broad
The Big Question:
Question: Which brand of paper towel is the most absorbent?
Hypothesis: Brand X is more absorbent than Brand Y
Formulate a Conclusion:
Flashlights run longer with "Ever Last" batteries.

Section 1.2: Scientific Equipment (page 10)
Microscope Diagram:
1. ocular lens   2. adjustment knob   3. arm
4. stage adjustment knob   5. base   6. mirror
7. stage   8. objective lenses   9. body tube
Microscope Matching:
1. c   2. d   3. e   4. f   5. g   6. h
7. b   8. a   9. i

Section 1.3: Scientific Measurement (page 12)
Converting Metric Units:
Try: 500 cm   Try: 0.02 m
Other Measurements (page 13)
Try: 240 min   Try: 3 wk
Vocabulary Building Activities (pages 14–15)
Appropriate Units of Measurement:
Length: 1. mm 2. m   3. cm   4. mm
Mass: 1. kg 2. kg 3. g   4. g
Fahrenheit and Celsius:
water boils: 212°F, 100°C
body temperature: 98°F, 40°C
room temperature: 70°F, 22°C
water freezes: 32°F, 0°C
Thermometers: Teacher check thermometers.
 1. 32°F   2. 22°C   3. -6.6°C

Chapter 2—Physcial Science Vocabulary
Section 2.1: Matter (pages 18–19)
Physical vs. Chemical Changes:
1. P   2. C   3. C   4. C   5. C   6. P
7. P   8. P   9. P   10. C   11. P   12. P
pH Scale:
battery acid (0.5), lemon juice (1.8), vinegar (3.0), orange juice (4.8), blood (7.2), sea water (8.0), ammonia (11.2), bleach (13.2), lye (14)
ph Values of Common Substances Table:
1. acid 2. base 3. base 4. acid 5. acid
6. base 7. acid 8. base 9. neutral
Mixtures vs. Compounds:
A mixture is the substance formed when two or more substances come together but do not combine to make a new substance. A compound is the new substance produced when two or more substances are chemically combined. Examples will vary.
Vocabulary Code Puzzle:
1. volume   2. gas   3. element
4. liquid   5. density
States of Matter:
Solids: fish, ice; Liquids: water, milk;
Gases: air in balloon, exhaust

Section 2.2: Energy (pages 22–23)
Heat Transfer:
1. radiation   2. conduction   3. convection
Forms of Energy:
1. electrical energy   2. thermal energy
3. sound energy   4. mechanical energy
5. mechanical energy
Magnetic Field:
1.   2.   3.

Light:
1. White light was separated into different colors
2. Because colors might appear blended, answers may vary. Possible answers include red, orange, yellow, green, blue, indigo, and violet.
3. Because colors might appear blended, answers may vary. Possible answers include red, orange, yellow, green, blue, indigo, and violet.
Mechanical Energy:
1. kinetic   2. potential   3. potential
4. potential   5. kinetic
Insulator or Conductor?:
1. insulator   2. conductor   3. insulator
4. insulator   5. conductor   6. conductor
7. insulator
Sound:
Sounds are vibrations in the form of waves. The vibration of the tuning fork caused the ping pong ball to move.
Circuits:
1. no   2. no   3. no   4. yes 5. no   6. yes

Section 2.3: Force and Motion (pages 26–27)
Machines:
1. screw   2. pulley   3. inclined plane
4. wedge   5. lever   6. wheel and axle
Resistance to Motion:
Activity #1 – heat
Activity #2 – no, The soap made the surface of the hands slippery and reduced friction.
The soap acted as a lubricant.

Answer Keys (cont.)

Lift:
The paper moved upward. The air moving over the top of the wing moves faster than air flowing under the wing. This causes an upward push on the wing and keeps birds in the air.

Venn Diagram:
Mass – the amount of matter in an object, not affected by gravity, measured with a balance scale
Weight – the amount of gravitational pull on an object, measured with a spring scale
Both – can be measured

Word Scramblers:
1. friction   2. buoyancy   3. pulley
4. mass   5. inertia

Chapter 3—Life Science
Section 3.1: Cells (pages 30–31)
Three Main Parts of a Cell:
1. nucleus   2. cell membrane   3. cytoplasm
Cell Review:
1. b   2. b   3. a
Venn Diagram:
Plant – cell wall, chloroplasts
Animal – no cell wall, no chloroplasts
Both – nucleus, cytoplast, cell membrane, Golgi bodies, mitochondria, vacuoles, ribosome, endoplasmic reticulum
The cell wall is a rigid structure outside the cell membrane that gives the plant support. Animals either have a skeleton or an exoskeleton for support.

Organisms:
Unicellular – an organism made up of only one cell
Muliticellluar – an organism made up of many cells
Examples will vary.

Section 3.2: Plants (pages 34–35)
Leaves:

Type of Leaves	Examples
simple leaf	
compound leaf	
	palmate pinnate

Leaf Veins	Examples
parallel veins	
net-veined leaves	

Seed Germination:
Seeds need water to provide nutrients for growth.
Sunlight and Photosynthesis:
The leaf was unable to receive sunlight to make food.
Chlorophyll:
1. Chlorophyll is green in color. It was released into the alcohol.
2. Chlorophyll gives plants their green color. In the fall, plants begin to go dormant and stop making new chlorophyll. The green chlorophyll disappears from the leaves. As the bright green fades away, other colors present in the leaves can be seen.

Parts of a Plant:
root – anchors the plant in the ground
stem – supports the plant and holds the leaves up to the light
leaf – makes food for the plant

Flower Parts:
1. anther   2. stigma   3. pollen grains
4. ovary   5. egg cells   6. filament
7. style

Seeds:
Dicot Seed – 1. embryo 2. seed coat 3. cotyledon
Monocot Seed – 1. seed coat 2. cotyledon 3. embryo

Section 3.3: Animals (pages 38–39)
Migration:
1. Monarch butterflies spend the summer in Canada and the Northern United States. They migrate as far south as Mexico for the winter.
2. Canadian geese fly south in the autumn to Florida and Mexico, and in the spring, they fly north to Canada.
3. Caribou travel from Canada to Alaska's Arctic National Wildlife Refuge.
4. Orioles fly south to Mexico and South America in fall and fly to North America in spring to lay eggs.
5. Manatees migrate in spring to the coasts of the Carolinas and to warmer Florida waters every fall.

Hibernation:
warm-blooded: bears, hamsters, mice, chipmunks, groundhogs, raccoons
cold-blooded: frogs, turtles, lizards, snakes, toads

Vertebrates:
Examples will vary.
fish – gills, lay eggs, cold-blooded
amphibians – most young have gills, most adults have lungs, lay eggs in water or moist ground, cold-blooded
reptiles – dry scaly skin, eggs have tough skin, cold-blooded
birds – feathers, wings, lay eggs, warm-blooded
mammals – hair at some point in life, young drink mother's milk, warm-blooded

Vertebrates vs. Invertebrates:
Examples will vary.
invertebrate – an animal that does not have a backbone
vertebrate – an animal that has a backbone

Section 3.4: Life Cycles (pages 42–43)
Metamorphosis:
egg, larva, pupa, adult
Frog Life Cycle:
 1. egg   2. larva (tadpole)   3. adult
Word Shape Puzzles:
 1. pupa   2. mammal   3. embryo
 4. chrysalis 5. larva
Plant:
 1. seed germinates
 2. plant grows to maturity
 3. plant flowers
 4. flower is pollinated and makes seeds
 5. seeds fall to the ground

Section 3.5: Ecology (pages 46–47)
Biomes: Examples will vary.
Forests – coniferous forests: usually cold winters and cool summers; deciduous forest: cold winters, warm, wet summers; tropical rain forests; warm, wet weather
Grasslands – steppes: dry areas; prairies: dry with some moisture; savannas: dry in winter and wet in summer
Deserts – very little rainfall
Aquatic – freshwater: lakes, rivers, and ponds; salt water: oceans and seas
Flow of Energy:
The population of animals eaten by the cat would increase, so eventually, the plants and animals they eat would decrease.
Ecosystem:
Examples will vary.
Producers – organisms that can make their own food
Consumers – organisms that get energy from eating plants and other animals
Decomposers – organisms that get energy from dead or decaying organisms

Chapter 4—Earth Science Vocabulary
Section 4.1: Weather (page 50)
Water Cycle Terms:
 1. precipitation   2. condensation
 3. precipitation   4. evaporation
Cloud Types:
 1. cumulus; big, scattered clouds with flat bottoms and round tops found about a mile above the earth; fair weather

 2. cirrus; made up of tiny ice crystals; white feathery-looking clouds; found very high in the sky, about five to ten miles up; possible change in weather soon
 3. stratus; cover the sky in a layer; rain and snow come from these clouds; found closer to earth, about 2,000 to 7,000 feet high; stormy weather
 4. cumulonimbus; tall and dark; rainstorm and possibly thunderstorms

Section 4.2: Seasons (page 52)
Earth's Tilted Axis:
 1. summer solstice   2. winter solstice
Seasons:
Dates are approximate.
 1. June 21, the Northern Hemisphere is tilted toward the sun, days are the longest of the year in Northern Hemisphere
 2. September 22, not tilted toward or away from the sun, lengths of day and night are the same all over Earth
 3. December 21, Northern Hemisphere is tilted away from the sun, the hours of daylight are shortest of the year in the Northern Hemisphere
 4. March 21, not tilted toward or away from the sun, lengths of day and night are the same all over Earth
Summer and Winter:

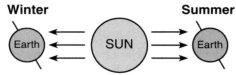

It is summer in the Southern Hemisphere when it is winter in the Northern Hemisphere.

Section 4.3: Rocks and Soil (page 55)
Crystals:
Salt crystals are cubic.
Earth's Surface:
 1. erosion   2. weathering   3. erosion
 4. erosion   5. weathering
Fossils:
Fossil C is the oldest. Soil is deposited in layers.
The deeper the layer, the older the soil deposit.
Rocks:
 1. sedimentary: created when layers of sediment settled to the bottom of the ocean and over thousands of years were pressed together, contains fossils; soft with layers; found where oceans or bodies of water once existed or still exist; chalk, coal, sandstone, shale, limestone

Answer Keys (cont.)

2. igneous: created when molten lava cools; glossy, crystalline, coarse-grained; found where volcanoes have existed; granite, basalt, obsidian, pumice, quartz

3. metamorphic: created when sedimentary or igneous rocks undergo a change due to pressure or heat within the earth; hard, crystals may appear, layers may develop; found deep in the earth where pressure and heat can affect the rocks; slate, marble

Section 4.4: Changes in the Earth's Surface (page 58)

Volcanoes:

1. cinder cone volcano – narrow bases and steep sides, formed when mainly cinder erupts from the central vent and piles up around it; Paricutin in Mexico

2. shield volcano – forms when lava erupts from several vents, spreads out widely, and builds up a dome shaped mountain; Mauna Loa in Hawaii

3. composite volcano – forms when both lava and cinder erupt from a central vent, the material piles up in alternate layers forming a cone shaped mountain; Mount Fuji in Japan

Earth's Layers:

1. crust – Earth's cool outer layer of mostly solid rock
2. mantle – Earth's vast middle layer of plastic-like and solid rock
3. outer core – melted iron and nickel
4. inner core – solid iron and nickel

Ring of Fire:

1. Indonesia   2. Japan   3. Hawaii
4. Alaska   5. Washington   6. Mexico
7. Argentina

Chapter 5—Space Science Vocabulary
Section 5.1: Objects in the Sky (page 61)

Halley's Comet:

1. nucleus   2. coma   3. tail

Constellations:

1. Cassiopeia   2. Big Dipper or Ursa Major
3. Canis Major   4. Draco   5. Orion
6. Gemini

Venn Diagram:

Meteor – an object usually ranging from the size of a dust particle to a rock that enters Earth's atmosphere; it burns up in Earth's atmosphere due to friction with the air; usually comes from comets

Meteorite – a meteor that is large enough to survive its passage through the atmosphere and hit the Earth; comes from asteroids; a few are from other planets or their moons

Both – objects from space

Section 5.2: Earth, Sun, and Moon (page 64)

Phases of the Moon:

1. New Moon   2. First Quarter   3. Full Moon
4. Third Quarter or Last Quarter

Eclipse:

1. solar eclipse   2. lunar eclipse

Sun:

1. photosphere   2. corona   3. sunspots
4. solar flare

Section 5.3: Solar System (page 67)

Solar System:

1. Mercury   2. Venus   3. Earth   4. Mars
5. Jupiter   6. Saturn   7. Uranus   8. Neptune

Space Exploration:

1961 Alan Shepard
1962 John Glenn
1965 Edward White
1969 Neil Armstrong and Edwin "Buzz" Aldrin
1972 Pioneer 10
1983 Sally Ride

Planet Facts:

Planet			
Mercury:	36 million miles	58.7 Earth-days
	88 Earth days	no moons
	no rings	
Venus:	67.2 million miles	243 Earth-days
	224.7 Earth-days	no moons
	no rings	
Earth:	93 million miles	23 hours, 56 minutes
	365.25 days	1 moon
	no rings	
Mars:	143 million miles	24 hours, 37 minutes
	687 Earth-days	two moons
	no rings	
Jupiter:	484 million miles	9 hours, 50 minutes
	11.9 Earth-years	62 moons
	rings	
Saturn:	887 million miles	10 hours, 39 minutes
	29.5 Earth-years	60 moons
	rings	
Uranus:	1,784 million miles	17 hours, 14 minutes
	84 Earth-years	27 moons
	rings	
Neptune:	2,794 million miles	16 hours, 7 minutes
	163.7 Earth-years	13 moons
	rings	

Pluto is no longer considered a planet. It has been reclassified a dwarf planet.

Bibliography

Beaver, John B. and Don Powers. *Electricity and Magnetism: Connecting Students to Science Series.* Quincy, Illinois: Mark Twain Media, Inc., 2003.

Beaver, John B. and Barbara R. Sandall. *Simple Machines: Connecting Students to Science Series.* Quincy, Illinois: Mark Twain Media, Inc., 2002.

Curtis, Mary E. and Ann Marie Longo. November 2001. *Teaching Vocabulary to Adolescents to Improve Comprehension.* International Reading Association. <http://www.readingonline.org/articles/curtis/>

Logan, LaVerne. *Rocks and Minerals: Connecting Students to Science Series.* Quincy, Illinois: Mark Twain Media, Inc., 2002.

Logan, LaVerne. *Sound: Connecting Students to Science Series.* Quincy, Illinois: Mark Twain Media, Inc., 2002.

Marzano, Robert and Debra J. Pickering. *Building Academic Vocabulary: Teacher's Manual.* ASCD, 2005.

Marzano, Robert. *Building Background Knowledge for Academic Achievement: Research on What Works in Schools.* ASCD, 2004.

Merriam-Webster Online. 7 May 2008. <http://www.merriam-webster.com/dictionary/chromat->

Powers, Don and John B. Beaver. *The Solar System: Connecting Students to Science Series.* Quincy, Illinois: Mark Twain Media, Inc., 2004.

Project G.L.A.D. February 20, 2007. Orange County Department of Education. <http://www.projectglad.com/>

Raham, Gary. *Science Tutor: Earth and Space Science.* Quincy, Illinois: Mark Twain Media, Inc., 2006.

Raham, Gary. *Science Tutor: Life Science.* Quincy, Illinois: Mark Twain Media, Inc., 2006.

Sandall, Barbara R. *Chemistry: Connecting Students to Science Series.* Quincy, Illinois: Mark Twain Media, Inc., 2002.

Sandall, Barbara R. *Light and Color: Connecting Students to Science Series.* Quincy, Illinois: Mark Twain Media, Inc., 2004.

Sciencesaurus: A Student Handbook. Houghton Mifflin, 2002.

Science Vocabulary Strategies Handbook. 2007–2008. <www.pscubed.org/documents/CompleteBook.pdf>

Shireman, Myrl. *Physical Science.* Quincy, Illinois: Mark Twain Media, Inc., 1997.